A SECRET JOURNAL

By

S. L. WILLIAMS

ISBN: 0-75961-579-9

This book is printed on acid free paper.

1stBooks – rev. 4/19/01

DEDICATION

Dedicated to the nondescript <u>others</u> who perished.

ACKNOWLEDGEMENT

I wish to thank the Grandson for entrusting me with the sacred family document, and giving me the latitude to recreate this story.

CHAPTER 1—A GIFT

My graduation from The Juilliard School of Music was a crowning achievement for me. It was the culmination of an arduous commitment. It was my personal affirmation that desire and determination can penetrate those imperceptible walls of deterrent. I had witnessed too many of my neighborhood friends being devoured by gangs, consumed by drugs, and ending up behind bars. My achievement was a testament to all kids of color that success is only a matter of "will."

My graduation ceremony was marred by the absence of my parents who had been snatched prematurely by the unbidden hands of death a few years earlier. My grandfather was the only living remnant of my family. He couldn't attend because of his losing battle with Alzheimer's Disease. So, alone, I graciously accepted my diploma and beamed for the cameras.

When I returned home from the ceremony, Grandpa was waiting with a chilled bottle of Dom Perignon. We made several toasts to my future success in music, then he gave me an old, tattered briefcase. It was similar to the one he always carried his sheet music in. I thought he'd written something new and wanted me to see it.

Opening the briefcase, I discovered the contents were not sheets of music—rather, an old, worn notebook with a smeared cover and words written in a foreign language that I didn't understand. I could read the name "Hermann Hoffmann," but it didn't ring any church bells because my grandpa's name was Herman Hoff.

"What is this, Grandpa?" I asked, afraid to venture into the scarred notebook.

"It's a journal of your grandpa's time in Hitler's concentration camp for Black Men."

"What!"

"Yes, son. This is the first time, in over forty years, this book has been opened. I wanted to present it to you and your father

1

together, but when he died I decided to wait until you became a man. Now, you're a college graduate and a man. I know you can handle what I have to tell you."

"You were in a concentration camp? I didn't know you were in the military."

"I wasn't in the military. Now, I want you to read through this stuff —it's written in English after the first few pages—then I want you to sit down with me, and I'll try to explain. It's best if you read first so you can comprehend when I tell you what happened."

I looked at my grandfather, and then at the thick notebook in my hand. My body quivered. It was like standing under a hot shower and suddenly, without warning, the hot water disappears and your body is peppered with melted ice. I had a compelling feeling that I was being deceived. Was this some weird joke Grandpa was trying to pull off? Who <u>was</u> this man sitting across from me? And who was Hermann Hoffmann? These questions bombarded me, and I reflected on the *real* grandfather I'd known.

My earliest, and most memorable recollection of the man who would later become a dominant influence on my life was his name: "Grandpa Herman." It was a name, like a lullaby, both soothing and inspirational. I eagerly awaited weekends when my father, mother, and I made the out-of-town excursions from Brooklyn to Hempstead, Long Island, to visit Grandpa Herman and Grandma Lucy. Grandpa would immediately sweep me up and saddle me across his broad shoulders. He was an imposing figure—tall, with bushy salt-n-pepper hair that was always neatly trimmed. He constantly pressed the reposing strands gently with his open palm to insure they remained in place.

He'd sit me on the piano stool beside him, my short legs swinging with pride, and I'd watch his lean, brown fingers glide gently over the black and white keys as if they were dear friends. His fingers seemed totally detached from his hands, and the sweet sound of music mesmerized me. I gloated at being his private audience.

During those years I felt my calling. The innate spirit had been awakened and I knew I was destined to play music like Grandpa Herman.

When I was around age five, Grandpa began coaching me on the piano. At age ten, I played piano, cello, and violin. In high school, I was a member of the band and played saxophone, clarinet, and oboe. However, during this delicate period of adolescence, I experienced a somber transformation. My parents were killed in an automobile accident.

My mother and father had been my whole universe. We did everything together as a family. My father would often surprise us with his abrupt suggestions for a drive to Philadelphia, Chicago, or St. Louis. and instantly, we were packing and off for the weekend or long holidays. My mother was an angel, so warm and caring. I could feel her lips brushing my forehead after I'd closed my eyes each night and before opening them each morning.

After the death of my parents, I moved to Hempstead to live with Grandpa Herman and Grandma Lucy. A year later, Grandma Lucy succumbed to cancer.

For the second time in my young life, I was confronted with the bare reality and vulnerability of life—of living—and the powerful, unyielding force of death. My entire lineage was slipping away. Just Grandpa and I were left in a family that I was so proud of. It was sadly odd, and a bit surreal, that three generations of Hoffs consisted of only five people. I never inquired about other relatives. My universe resided with my immediate family.

My grandfather refilled my glass of wine, and I was jarred back into reality. I fingered the notebook in my hand, looked at my grandfather through the bottom of my empty glass, and said goodnight.

CHAPTER 2—THE REVELATION

That night I lay in the quiet, foreboding darkness of my bedroom, contemplating my course of action. I wanted to open the tattered notebook lying on the night table near my bed because I was curious. I wanted to understand precisely what my grandfather meant by, "It's a journal of your grandpa's time in Hitler's concentration camp." Conversely, I was terrified at what my curiosity might uncover. Since my grandfather had not been in the military, the only other explanation was he had to be Jewish. For me it was logical; everything I'd read or viewed on the Holocaust was about Jews being slaughtered by Hitler. Gypsies were the only other ethnic group mentioned in historical data of the Holocaust, so it was incomprehensible for me to believe that Black People were among the eleven million victims of the Holocaust.

I turned on the light, sat up, and reached for the notebook. Some pages were crisp, as if they had been baked in a hot oven. The handwriting was without a doubt that of my grandfather. I always admired the artistry of his long, flowing strokes, interspersed with short alphabetical jabs as he inserted an a, crossed a t, or dotted an i. There were no dates, only three pages written in what I guessed was German. I started reading the first page written in English.

My name is Hermann Hoffmann. I was born on 9 June 1925 near Hamburg, Germany. I'm writing this in hopes someone will read it after I'm gone and understand what happened to me and many other African males under Hitler's reign of terror. I have no family. My mother died giving me life. My father was out with Jewish friends during the "Night of Broken Glass," and never returned.

My father was professor of history and philosophy at Hamburg University. Bought off a slave ship from Ghana when he was ten by a Duke in Germany, he was later raised in royalty.

He attended the best schools, studying language, natural history, and art.

When my father was thirty, he married an African servant. The marriage was arranged by the family he lived with. They had one child—me. I was raised in the seaport town of Wilhelmsburg, near Hamburg. As I said, my mother died giving me life, so I never felt the soft and loving hands, the happy smiles, and the warm hugs that mothers are famous for. Having never experienced them, I didn't miss them. But, I had pictures of my mother all over our house. Whenever I felt sad and wanted to cry, I would imagine her holding and kissing me. It made everything better.

My father and I lived in the same house where I was born. It was part of the pension he received from the Duke. We did many things together, but one of the most memorable times was our trip to Berlin for the 1936 Olympics.

After reading the first page, I fell asleep. It was interesting and provocative. And, although I couldn't immediately identify with the 'slaves being raised in royalty' bit, I could hear my grandfather's voice resonating through the words, and felt the validity in what he was saying. My comprehension of the page was abated because I wanted and needed a better introduction from my grandfather. My initial impression of the journal was: the beginning of an emotional, and educational journey into a dark and unbidden past. I felt like a person about to make a world-shaking discovery. Just the thought of a secret being suppressed for over forty years, and suddenly I was about to be the sole, uncontested recipient of its contents, was awesome. I yielded my subconscious mind to sort everything out while I slept.

I awoke the next morning fresh and energized. Whatever happened during my hours of sleep must have been positive. Mentally, I had prepared a list of questions I wanted to ask my grandfather. But when I looked into his room he was sound asleep, and I didn't want to wake him. Since his illness had been

5

diagnosed as Alzheimer's disease, he'd experienced many sleepless nights. Sometimes he walked the floor most of the night. Whenever I attempted to sit with him and talk, or do other things to detract from his illness, he would make me go to bed. Those were nights that I dragged to my room feeling useless. But, since the introduction of the notebook, my speculation was that perhaps the notebook, more so than his illness, was the culprit of his chronic unrest. Now that he was making a conscientious effort to raked back the cobwebs of his past, he was more relaxed and able to sleep.

Following Grandma Lucy's death, I'd tried to spend as much time with Grandpa as possible. We had standard routines that made our times together more interesting and enjoyable. Mornings, we ate breakfast together. I usually prepared breakfast because I did my jogging early and was the first one up. Lunch, depended on our individual schedules. If we were home, we had lunch together. In the evenings, we alternated being chef-for-the-day and enjoyed a full meal. Normally, after the meal we'd watch Larry King or some other anchor person analyzing the news. But this particular evening we sat quietly; the TV turned off, the tattered notebook opened across my lap. It was a somber period—as if we were both afraid to open the door and step into a long and harried past.

"Well, did you read it?" My grandfather asked.

" Yeah. Read the first page."

"Only the first page?"

"Yes. I was confused about a few things. I guess what I need is a better introduction, more explanation, or some focus so I can fully understand what this whole thing is really all about."

"Okay. What didn't you understand?"

"Why did you keep this ... *secret* hidden for so long?"

Wordless, he stared at me. Then dropping his head, he spoke.

"Self-preservation, I guess. When the American soldiers liberated our camp they were perplexed at seeing a group of

Black Men locked up together, and to amplify the confusion, most of us spoke only German.

"Our liberators were all white soldiers and I remember hearing one soldier speak very candidly about the situation. "Goddam! I didn't know there was such a thing as a Black German."

"I spoke English because my father was a staunch advocate of Liberal Arts studies, and encouraged me to study language in school. English was my first choice and I was fluent. So, I got this wild idea, while the American soldiers stormed the camp shooting and yelling in English, that maybe I could pretend to be an American expatriate caught up in the war. They believed me when I told them I was a musician from New York and was arrested by the Nazis on my way back to America. I had no identification, other than the eloquent command of their language, so they put me on a ship to New York."

"But Grandpa, you'd never been to America before. How did you pull it off?"

"When I arrived in New York—Ellis Island—everyone was so caught up in a frenetic euphoria because the war against Hitler had ended. It was quite easy to assimilate into the mainstream of American society. I told many lies about when and where I was born, invented new parents, and obviously no one checked. Everyone was aware of what Hitler had done to the Jews, and I guess they empathized with me.

"Later, I was issued a social security card, passport, and associated documents that made me a citizen of the United States. The lies soon became a reality, and I had to live with them, face deportation to Africa, or spend time in jail. I knew no one in Africa, and going to jail was unthinkable. It's such a relief now that I can finally tell the truth."

"Grandpa, you say my great grandfather was bought as a slave and raised in royalty. How can that be?"

"Yes, I know it's difficult to comprehend, but you have to understand the history of slavery in Europe—especially in Germany—"

"But the definition of a *slave* is one who is bound in servitude as an instrument of labor. Was my great grandfather bought as a slave and later adopted by a royal family?"

"Not quite. Slavery was open to interpretation by those involved in the slave trade. Between years 1700—1900, thousands of *Mohrens* (German for Negroes) were carried from their home country(mostly from the cape coast castle off the coast of Ghana) where they had been captured and segregated according to gender and age. European royalty found it sporting to dabble in the slave trade. Children had the greatest value, as big-eyed dolls with turbans and magnificent clothing. Nice black angels. Most of the slaves in Germany worked as pages or army musicians and were integrated into German society. The most popular slave trade with German royalty was boys between the ages of ten and twelve. They were bought, baptized, and became members of the family.

"European slaves—especially in Germany— were lifted to the higher level of their owners. The *Mohr* prestige was the same prestige as their royal and wealthy citizen owners."

"What did they do ... I mean, how did they function, or make the transition from slave to Royal Family Member?"

"Remember, the most popular trade was young boys. Their cognitive skills were not fully developed, and most of their assignments were to hold the umbrella, serve and sleep in the same room as their master. This close proximity created an atmosphere for learning and future development. An older *Mohr*, would serve as a personal servant or as a military musician. It was a privilege profession with a salary and pension. *Mohrens* had a roof over their heads, regular meals, and decent clothing. Most German citizens at that time could only dream of such treatment."

"How can we explain such wide disparity between the treatment of European and American slaves?"

"Europeans had a more direct dealing with African slaves during the furor of colonization. They were a constant witness to the proud and resilient nature of the Africans as they fought to preserve their homeland against European expansion. The Germans, for instance, learned a valuable lesson that obviously Hitler didn't bother to read about, or perhaps with his limited educational background, couldn't comprehend."

Grandpa saw the puzzled look on my face and realized that Hitler wasn't the only person ignorant of the colonization of Africa.

"Okay, I'll give you a brief background." He said with a broad grin.

"Prince Bismarck, then the chief minister of Imperial Germany, was at first indifferent to creating colonies as emblems of national prestige as other European countries were scrambling to do. Germany was already the leading economic country, however, under pressure of commercial interest from port cities like Hamburg and Bremen for the potential goods and raw materials, he soon changed his mind as he watched other European powers edging toward territorial acquisition.

"So, in 1884, Bismarck suddenly announced protectorates in South West Africa, Cameroon, and Togo.

"Having gained a colonial empire in Africa, Germany undertook the administration of her African holdings. However, Germany was unprepared to administer the newly won territories and was guided toward a policy of expediency of products, which relied heavily on arbitrary and coercive methods of labor recruitment. A total lack of experienced personnel led to a system of indirect rule through local chiefs and contractual agreements. These officials were sometimes guilty of ruthless enforcement—a line of conduct that added fresh unrest to chronic outbreaks of violence by the Africans against German rule.

"For twenty years, the German administration in East Africa had to wage warfare to achieve peace through African submission. Estimates indicate that at least seventy thousand Africans perished, many from disease and malnutrition, in 1907 at a place we know of today as Rwanda. Germany was unofficially accused of genocide.

"After the war in East Africa, Germany developed a more liberal regime and concentrated on reform and economic expansion—missionary schools and public health services were encouraged. The arbitrary corporal punishment of Africans practiced in former times gave way to formalized judicial procedures.

"By the eve of the First World War, Germany's administration had overcome many of its former limitations and converted an unsettled land, plagued by slaving and chronic warfare, to a peaceful colony with an expanding economy. Germany became paternalistic over its East Africa colony until it was turned over to British and Belgian rule under the Peace of Versailles and League of Nations at the end of WWI.

"Germany learned that domination and oppression were not the solution to a peaceful coexistence, but respect and mutual understanding of basic human rights and values were."

"Where did you learn all this stuff, Grandpa? I studied American and European history, and I don't remember reading anything about all this stuff you're telling me."

"Well, history books are carefully chosen by schools for specific educational agenda, but I suspect most schools with an African studies curriculum will give you an insight into some of the things we're discussing."

"Okay, so far I'm beginning to weave through some of the mystery. You said your father disappeared one night after going out with Jewish friends. What was the 'Night of Broken Glass?'"

"My father had many friends and colleagues at the University, but most were Jews. In the early thirties, Jews made up about one percent of the German population. Most civil service jobs, university and court positions, and other professional areas of public life, were held by Jews. When Hitler started implementing his racial ideology theory, he enacted new laws that forced Jews to quit their jobs and positions of power. Some of those laws were so severe that it made daily life very difficult for them. They couldn't attend public schools, go to the theater, reside, or even walk in certain sections of German cities.

"Even though my father wasn't directly affected by the new laws, he refused to abandon his friends. The Night of Broken Glass, also known as *Kristallnacht*, in 1938, stemmed from the assassination of a German diplomat in Paris by a young Polish Jew. It was a centrally organized riot. The destruction of Synagogues, Jewish-owned homes, the arrest of Jewish men and the murder of others followed. I remember waiting at home for my father, hoping and praying he was okay. I could see flames rising high above the city, lapping at the sky over burning buildings and Jewish homes. I could hear the woeful screams above the gaudy wails of fire engines and the violent shattering of glass. It was a horrifying night that is permanently etched in my mind, and it will only leave when I close my eyes for the last time."

CHAPTER 3—BASTARD MUSIC

The next day, following the emotional evening about slavery in Germany, and the infamous Night of Broken Glass, I received a phone call to report to the local high school for an interview with the principal concerning my application for music teacher. I fought to quell my excitement, but deep inside I knew I had been selected for the job. My grandfather cautioned me not to get my hopes up too high.

"If you don't get this one, there will be others," he'd said before I left home."

This was to be my first real job in music. I needed some practical work experience—teaching music— before pursuing my master's at Juilliard. Although I had sufficient funds from my parents estate to pay for my schooling, I wanted to try to pay my way from my own earnings. The local high school was only a short distance from our house, which was convenient if Grandpa's illness required emergency care.

I walked into the school brimming over with confidence.

"Mr. Saberstein will see you now," the receptionist said, with a warm smile, after returning to her desk.

I interpreted her smile as a welcome gesture.

"Please sit down, Mr. Hoff." Mr. Saberstein indicated a plush chair in front of his huge mahogany desk.

The walls of his office were covered with certificates and plaques, most with his name in bold letters or his photograph flashing a happy smile.

"I'm impressed with your qualifications, Mr. Hoff. Notwithstanding the fact you've had no experience as a teacher of music. However, we take great pride in our policy of hiring young, talented people who can adapt easily and will follow our strict principles of teaching."

I tried not to read into the 'will follow' part, but I couldn't ignore the sudden tug of my conscience string conveying that something was wrong. It was like walking into a room full of noisy people, and the moment you cross the threshold a quaint silence spreads rapidly throughout the room.

"Mr. Hoff, there is one question on the application that is of particular interest to us. It asks the type of music that interests you most. You listed jazz among your interest. Are you deeply involved with jazz?"

The question floated while I stared at the base of his desk. I wasn't prepared to give an answer because I didn't know where he was going. I could feel his gaze piercing me and my mouth opened to exhale. "I like many different types of music and I think my interest is equally shared." I blurted, and immediately knew it was the wrong answer by his facial expression.

"Mr. Hoff. Our student body is somewhat diverse, but our music is not.

We teach directly from the masters: Bach, Beethoven, Irving Berlin, etc... . We feel very strongly that this is basic, and the only form of music for our students. No Latin, blues, jazz, or other off-colored music."

I felt another tug at my conscience string, but ignored the room full of people, "No Duke Ellington, no Count Basie?" I knew the answer before I asked.

"Absolutely not! Our last music teacher insisted, over my explicit instructions against integrating bastard music into our curriculum, on letting the students experiment with weird forms of bastard music. His contract was not renewed. We have since included my instructions as an integral part of our contract."

I fought the impulse to get up and walk out. This man was totally biased about music. How could I work for him. But I thought about the students and the ongoing programs to keep music in the school, and I felt obligated to do my part. Besides, I was curious to see the diverse student body he mentioned. My conscience string could be sending me the wrong message, I thought.

"You think you can conform to our strict rules on the type of music we want taught in our school, Mr. Hoff?"

"Yes sir. I don't see any problems." I lied and immediately hated myself.

"Good! Welcome to Central High School."

CHAPTER 4—THE OLYMPIC GAMES

My grandfather was elated that I had been accepted by the high school to teach music. It was his ardent desire that I become a professor and teach at Juilliard. I didn't tell him about my dismal disappointment with the interview. Mr. Saberstein was certainly biased about certain types of music, but I didn't know how deep-rooted his feelings were. When he blatantly declared jazz and blues bastard music, I was obliged to explore his feelings further. Telling my grandfather about it would only infuriate him, so I packed it deep inside and rejoiced with him.

"Here's a letter from Germany for you," he said, passing me the letter that flashed a happy smile on my face. "I didn't know you knew anyone in Germany."

"Yeah, a former classmate of mine who lives in Berlin—an exchange student."

"Oh, that's great. Tell me more about your friend later."

"Okay, Grandpa."

I went to my room and hastily opened the letter from Sigrid. We'd met during my last year at Juilliard. We had the same curriculum, enjoyed the same types of music, and formulated the same plans for our future in music. We dated several times and enjoyed each other's company. Actually, she was the first girl I'd ever dated. Music had consumed all my time and interest, and I didn't realize, until I met Sigrid, that there were other things in life worthy of commitment. I kept the relationship secret, partially because I didn't want to share her with anyone else, and because I didn't know how to tell my grandfather that I was having a relationship with a foreign girl who happened to be white.

While reading the letter, a feeling of warmth and comfort covered me, like a light blanket on a cool spring morning, and I knew instantly from the vibes bouncing off her words, that the relationship was more than casual. When she said she and her parents were coming to New York during the summer and they were looking forward to meeting me, the feeling mushroomed. I felt weightless—as if I was floating somewhere in space.

Time drifted while I sat holding the letter and feeling a heroic sense of greatness. I had found a girl who cared enough to write me a letter.

But my euphoria ended abruptly when I thought about my grandfather and the journal. I wondered if he harbored any ill feelings toward Germans. There was so much I didn't understand about Hitler and the Germans. Now that Sigrid was coming back into my life, and because my grandfather was treated badly by the Germans, I wanted to pick up the journal and read.

The day we left for Berlin was one of joy and wonder. I had never been out of Hamburg—to the best of my knowledge. And the flight aboard a Lufthansa airplane was thrilling. I sat holding my father's hand and looking out the small window at the earth below. It was a magnificent sight. I thought of how much God must enjoy his view as he looks down on his marvelous creation. It was a time in my life when I felt I was beginning to understand what life was really all about. I was almost a teenager—very active in sports, track and field being my favorite. I was on my way to see one of the greatest sporting events in the world, and to witness competition between the world's greatest athletes. To compete in the Olympics was my dream and the dreams of all my friends. It was the ultimate sporting event.

Riding in a taxi from Templehof airport, the view of the city was spectacular. Red, white, and black was the dominant color scheme. The massive buildings, along tree-lined boulevards, were draped with majestic banners. Huge swastika flags were planted along the boulevards and diffused with mounted oil paintings of special German towns and cities. Hundreds of flags from nations competing in the games were flying everywhere in commemoration of this special event. The towering Brandenberg gate, with its galloping chariot, was covered with green garlands and swastika flags. Everywhere, the city glowed with fresh new paint.

The most memorable of all the sites we'd seen was the new Olympic Stadium. It was a massive stone structure that resembled a gigantic spaceship hovering for takeoff. Red cinder brick glistened in the sunlight. A plush carpet of green grass bordered each side of the structure, and inside, dusty grey stones rose tier upon tier to encompass seats for over 100,000 people.

On the first day, light rain fell while we stood in a long line to enter the stadium. The scene outside was festive. Loud music blared as soldiers marched with colors flipping in the breeze. The most dramatic moments on that first day were: the arrival of the torch, arrival of Hitler, hoisting flags of competing nations, toll of the great bell, and the simultaneous release of thousands of pigeons that flew away, carrying colored ribbons representing the competing nations.

As we moved into our seats, I could see the quiet anticipation of the crowd. They were waiting to see the young black student from Ohio University, Jessie Owens. His incredible feats of equaling one world record and breaking three others, had preceded him. He was indeed the focus of attention. For most of the young boys like myself who had an intense interest in sports, he was a hero. Because he was black, like me, he was my "personal" hero.

The crowd chanted "Yesseh ... Yesseh, Owens," as they waited impatiently for his heat to begin. I saw him enter the track. He had a beautiful, well-proportioned body, and he stood tall. My chest heaved with pride. He looked like a black Greek god.

Once the race was underway, the crowd roared as Owens swept down the track like a whirlwind, winning by yards and equaling the world and Olympic record of 10.3 seconds. During the second race, with 100,000 eyes glued to him, Owens electrified the stadium by storming through to win in the unbelievable time of 10.2 seconds.

Everywhere we went after the first day of the Olympics, people were discussing Jessie Owen. When my father and I approached, they became more animated and spoke openly to us.

We were proud to be black. That was the first and last time I can remember being so proud of who I was.

Several days later, the proud feeling turned to rage. The men's 100 meter final was, although we didn't know at the time, the beginning of Hitler's public vilification for the Black Man. The six runners included two blacks and four whites. One runner was German, and although everyone wanted Germany to win at least one track medal, it was obvious he had little chance against Owens. Owens ran the race at a devastating speed equaling the Olympic and world records again.

Then it happened. Hitler was in the honor box to receive a group of winners. A German athlete for the Hammer was first, and Owens was the second athlete to enter the dais in front of Hitler. The German athlete was crowned; he stood straight and gave Hitler the Nazi salute. The music for "Deutschland Uber Alles" was played as the crowd joined singing. Like a million steel rods piercing the sky, right hands throughout the stadium shot outward in salute. Owens was next. He was crowned, and as the band played the "Star Spangled Banner," Owens bowed to Hitler who turned abruptly and walked away. There was a hushed silence throughout the stadium. The reaction of the crowd wasn't so much a disapproval of Hitler for snubbing Owens because he was black, rather, because Owens was the greatest athlete of the game.

I felt deep anger, and for the first time in my young life, I was introduced to hate. That despicable little man with the weighted black mustache had insulted me, my hero, my father, and all black people in the world. I guess it was a blessing that I was only a little boy, because had I been a man, I would've been shot for trying to squeeze the life out of him with my bare hands. My father must have seen the hurt and anguish in my face when he asked if I was ready to go home. We left, and I noticed my father held his head high, but the lines in his face were taut, and I could detect the disappointment and outrage in his voice.

The pungent smell of food invaded my room, and I knew Grandpa was preparing my favorite dish for dinner—lasagna. When I entered the kitchen he was humming a tune as he busily placed dishes on the table.

"I was just getting ready to call you to open a bottle of wine." He said.

"Red or white?"

"Red. I noticed your friend in Germany is named S. Schiller. That's a traditional German name. What's his first name?"

"Sigrid." I said without hesitation. There was a loud silence. Only the subdued popping sound of the cork easing from the wine bottle made me realize what I had just said.

"Oh! Sigrid, huh. Is she a nice girl?"

"Yeah, she is very nice." The sound from my throat came in gasps, as if I were recovering from a choking seizure. "Ah... we have a lot in common; the same interest in music, same goals in life, we enjoy each other and—"

"You never mentioned her before... Why were you keeping her a secret?"

"I don't know. I really don't know." I felt waves of guilt weaving through my body. I had planned to tell him... now he felt I didn't trust him. I didn't want that... .

"Did you think I wouldn't approve of her because she is German?"

I looked at my grandfather for the first time since I'd mentioned Sigrid's name.

"Maybe." I uttered. It was an utterance of hope that my grandfather would understand without having me blunder through an explanation.

"Look, son. What happened to me in Germany had nothing to do with the German people. Ordinary Germans were friendly and hospitable by nature, and would never persecute Jews, Blacks, or anyone else on their own accord had they not been incited to do so by Hitler, their crazed leader."

"What was the racial attitude toward mixed marriages or relationships during that time, Grandpa?"

"Hitler's racial ideology advocated selective breeding to improve the human race. All mixed relationships were forbidden. Incentive programs were established for *pure* Germans to produce children. In contrast, a sterilization program was passed into law to reduce the number of genetic inferiors."

"Sterilization? You mean they castrated people?"

"Yes. Radiation was also used. Gypsies and Blacks were main targets, and they were prohibited from intermarrying with Germans. Children of mixed African/German racial background were also sterilized."

"Did you ever have a German girlfriend, Grandpa?"

"No. But I had a relationship with a German woman whose husband was missing on the same night as my father. She was much older. We were very close. She looked after me after my father disappeared, and at times protected me from the Nazis who were openly searching for black males to implement another one of Hitler's sinister programs. She was a sweet lady and perhaps, if things had been different, I might have married her and you wouldn't be sitting here asking me all these questions. So, let's eat."

Later, as we drank coffee and savored the tasty apple strudel cake that Grandpa was so fond of, I spoke for the first time since we'd started dinner.

"Grandpa, do you know of any other cases, besides your own, where Blacks in Germany suffered simply because they were black?"

"Yes, several, but there were two incidents that I will always remember because they received a lot of media attention. A black wrestler named Jim Wango, was extremely popular and had a huge following in International Professional Wrestling contests, where he beat one white wrestler after another. One night, while wrestling in Nuremberg—the town where he lived with his German wife—the match was stopped by a sports minister from the Third Reich. Newspapers quoted the minister as saying:

"'In sports involving strength, we approve. What we are opposed to is the linking of sports with dirty business interests and sales gimmicks. It is a sales gimmick, an appeal to inferior people, to subhumans, to put a Negro on view and let him compete with white people. It is not in the spirit of the people of Nuremberg to let white men be subdued by a Black Man. Anyone who applauds when a Black Man throws a white man of our blood to the ground is no Nuremberger.'

"Wango was finally banned from wrestling in Germany. He was also boycotted in the town of Nuremberg. The town merchants refused to sell him food. He became ill and a Nazi doctor wouldn't admit him to a hospital. His manager, in frustration, took him to a hospital in Berlin. He was diagnosed with a severe kidney ailment. He died a few hours after being admitted.

"But the racial attitude of black and white competitors changed when Max Schmeling won a victory over Joe Louis a few months before the Olympic games. Schmeling was given a hero's welcome when he returned home to Germany. The Third Reich-controlled media responded by saying:

"'It was more than a boxing match. Here black and white confronted each other, and all the foes of Nazi Germany, whatever their color, reckoned on the overthrow of the German. It was not Joe Louis that was defeated. The great masses of our people believed that Max Schmeling saved the reputation of the white race. His victory was a question of prestige for our race. With his hard fists, he has won the respect of the world for the German nation.'

"Later, when Joe Louis knocked out Schmeling in their return bout, the same press explained:

"'The American was a wild monster from the jungle, who knows how to beat white men by a barrage of cheating blows to the liver.'

"Yes, those were some frustrating times for the Black Man in Germany."

"Grandpa, I've just finishing reading the journal entry about your trip to Berlin to see the 1936 Olympics."

"Good!"

"Well, as usual, I have some disturbing questions."

"Shoot!"

"Was the whole world oblivious to what was going on in Germany? Countries bordering Germany must have been aware of a Nazi uprising. Was there no concern for Human Rights Violations? And with all the other flagrant violations, why did the World Olympic Committee allow the Games to he held in Berlin?"

"Hold on, son. You're throwing too much at me. One thing at a time. First, the whole world didn't really *know* what was going on in Germany. There were lots of suspicion but few facts. The Nazis had complete control over the information media: radio, newspapers, and foreign journalists. Nothing was printed or broadcast without the approval of the information minister from the Third Reich. Everyone treated Hitler and his henchmen as comical rather than dangerous. It was a political comedy skit that most Germans and perhaps the rest of the world felt would have a short run.

"The Olympic committee could not prove Human Rights Violations, even though there were no Jews or Blacks competing from Germany. Germany's official reply was: no one qualified. Some countries, including the United States, resisted but finally sent teams to participate after Germany made concessions by adding several Jewish participants."

"What was Hitler's response to his snubbing of Jessie Owens?"

"He *never* gave a public apology, but privately he was quoted as saying, "'The Americans should be ashamed of themselves, letting Negroes win their medals.'

"'Do you think I will allow myself to be photographed shaking hands with a Negro?'"

"And how did you feel personally, Grandpa?"

"I was young but deeply hurt. I remember crying all the way home. We rode the train back to Hamburg, and my father held me as he stared absently out the window. He didn't try to explain. He simply tried to wipe away the rapid flow of tears rolling down my face. I think that was the day I became a man."

CHAPTER 5—A NIGHT OF TERROR

Several days after the Olympic games ended, Germany's news media heaped lavish praises on the German athletes for superior performances. Germany won the most medals—180. Second was the United States with 124. For the Third Reich it was a resounding success. Not one word was mentioned about Jessie Owens and his four gold medals. But the phenomenal performances of Jessie Owens and the other black athletes on his team obviously worried Hitler. He realized the showcasing his superior Aryan athletes to the world had been thwarted by Black Men. Deep inside his wanton, and jingoistic mind, he was planning revenge.

My father and I didn't talk much about the Olympic games after we came home. We tried to resume our lives as they were before we left for Berlin. But it was different at school. Most of the kids in our athletic program wanted to be like Jessie Owens. They were more dedicated and worked harder trying to reach the level of excellence he had demonstrated at the games. Assumptions were made that all colored athletes had abnormal muscular qualities different from those of whites. In particular, an "elongated heel," which gave us extra spring, and therefore an unfair advantage in track and field. Because I was black like Jessie Owens, my friends constantly asked if it were true. I had no reply. They demanded I display my feet and heel for their inspection. I obliged simply to prove my feet were the same as theirs. I don't know whether they were convinced, but it certainly changed their attitude.

In the meantime, another problem was surfacing at school which signaled the onset of the Holocaust. Most of the Jewish teachers—over half the teaching staff—suddenly stopped showing up for work. The remaining teachers: Germans, a few Africans, and others, were trying to carry on—teaching more classes than normal. This led to the abrupt cancellation of many subjects. Mr. Klein, my music teacher, was one of those teachers who had departed. The music school was closed, which was particularly frustrating for me because music and athletics were really the only reasons I wanted to go to school.

Frau Benz, my next door neighbor, was also a teacher at the school, and she had a rich background in music. She agreed to teach me music until the school reopened. Her husband and my father were colleagues at the university. I overheard them talking one night.

"If Hitler continues his persecution of Jews, our whole society will crumble," my father said.

"Yes, its not only an irreplaceable brain drain, it's also a cultural calamity." Herr Benz remarked.

"You know Karl, something has to be done before we're caught up in a crisis that will never end until our society is totally destroyed. Now, you are German. How do you explain what is happening here?"

"A simple answer. We let a psychopath from Austria creep into our mind, and he made some of us believe that we were better than anyone else in the world. Because we were at a period of such low esteem, we were gullible. In 1933, when he became chancellor, we tried to wake up, but it was too late."

"Yes, I remember you and I discussing it when his party won a majority of seats in the Reichstag. We said Germany was in for a fast roller coaster ride. But man, people are being beaten on the streets and some killed for no apparent reason. Your friends and mine are being set up for mass extermination. Who will be next?"

"Well, my friend. You are African but a German citizen—"

"So are the Jews. Some were here before Hitler brought his twisted ass over from Austria. Look what he did at the Olympic games with Jessie Owens. I was there, Karl. My son saw it. How can I explain to my son how the demented mind of one man can control the lives of millions of people? My son is black. He knows he is different, but dammit, he was born here! He has a right to grow up and be a man."

"I'm a German, a citizen ... a so-called Aryan, but the SS, or the Gestapo wouldn't hesitate to shoot me down if I made any public statements against the man that has promised to lead Germany out of economic woes, and make us shine against the rest of the world.

"Let's face it, you being Black is not part of the correlation. Just being in Germany is the problem."

"Well, Karl, what can we do?"

"I don't know. Whatever we do we'll be risking our lives. But we must do something."

This conversation between Herr Benz and my father happened only a week before their disappearance.

The conversation I overheard also created a lot of internal problems for me. They talked about things I didn't understand. I didn't dare ask my father because I didn't want him to know I had been listening. He always told me it was impolite to listen to others talk without being physically present and a participant in the conversation. I just couldn't visualize a person killing another person for "no apparent reason." What I did reason was that the man from Austria and Hitler were the same. Seeing him at the Olympics was the second time I'd been in the same stadium with him.

My school went to Hannover to compete in a Junior Olympics. I was too young to participate, but I went along to support my friends. I provided water, towels, and moral support. Kids came from all over Germany. On the last day a lot of excitement was generated about the Fuhrer's arrival. Finally, a long line of automobiles drove into the stadium. When he stepped out of the open car, the stadium echoed with Heil Hitler! Heil Hitler! And the sound of young voices reverberated in a deafening chant, as if God had stepped from heaven to mingle with his flock.

He spoke to us, but it was difficult understanding what he was saying. He sounded as if he were screaming the same words over and over like an impaired record. All my friends were beaming with joy after he'd left. I beamed, too, but felt nothing.

When we returned to Hamburg, many of my friends talked about joining Youth Groups. Some were already members, but no one had asked me to join. I wasn't really concerned until the day a friend gave me a leaflet. His parents had made him join. The leaflet read:

It is on youth that the future of the German nation depends. Hence, it is necessary to prepare the entire German Youth for its coming duties. The government therefore pass the following law:

1. The entire German Youth within the borders of the Reich is organized in the Hitler Youth.
2. It is not only in home and school, but in the Hitler Youth as well that all of Germany's Youth be educated physically, mentally, and morally, in the spirit of National Socialism, to serve the nation and the racial community.

When my father saw the leaflet, he sat me down to talk.

"This is not for you, son. I know you feel bad that your friends are joining, but this is just not for you. These Youth Groups are not all about athletics. They are programs set up to train young athletes to become soldiers."

"But I want to be a good athlete like Jessie Owens," I protested.

"I know, but believe me, this is not the place to be like Jessie Owens. What you need to do is stick with your music. Music is the future for you."

I was disappointed but knew my father was right. I could never become a part of the Youth Groups because I didn't have the same enthusiasm as my friends. So, music became my priority. My father bought sheet music and records from Paul Robeson, who was performing in Hollywood musicals, Louis Armstrong, Sidney Bechet, Count Basie, Cab Calloway, and Duke Ellington. Suddenly, I discovered other heroes to occupy my time and help me to maintain focus. But another alarming situation that became a detractor was occurring at my school. I noticed that most of the black students had stopped coming to school.

My father said, "Oh, their fathers probably found jobs in other countries and moved their families. It's quite normal because good jobs are hard to find in Germany."

I hesitated to believe my father because some of those students were good friends, and they wouldn't just leave without saying goodbye. Anyway, I tried not to be overly concerned about other extraneous matters as I plunged headlong into my music studies. But sometimes, in the streetcar on my way home from school, kids would whisper and point at me. Then after getting off the streetcar, soldiers would yell at me as I walked the five hundred meters to my house: "Rhineland Bastard, Rhineland Bastard."

I didn't understand what they were saying, or even if the words applied to me. I spoke to no one about it. Despite all the taunting harassment, life was fairly normal until "Kristallnacht."

It was a calm November evening. A light fog covered our town, caressing buildings, and flirting with street lamps. I had just finished my music lessons with Frau Benz and was walking out of her house when I noticed people gathering in groups along the street. Some were yelling and raising their fists in mock defiance. I couldn't understand what they were screaming about, but obviously Frau Benz, who was standing in her doorway, did.

"Go inside your house Hermann. Lock the doors," she yelled after me.

I rushed inside, hoping my father was home. The house was empty. I didn't know what was going on, but from the disquieting reaction of Frau Benz, it wasn't good.

I sat by the window watching the crowd work themselves into a fanatical frenzy. When I saw them waving burning flares in the air, I turned away from the window. My concern was for my father, and I went to my bedroom to await his arrival.

Somewhere between the noisy crowd outside and the comfort of my bedroom, I fell asleep.

The next morning, Frau Benz came over to inquire if my father had returned. He had not. Her husband was also missing. He had been with my father and friends early in the evening. They'd left together to attend a faculty meeting at the university.

Throughout the morning we sat listening to the radio, hoping and praying that someone knew what had happened to our loved ones. But to our unsettling dismay, all we heard were repetitive news broadcasts about the cowardly assassination in Paris and who was to blame. I didn't care about all that. I just wanted my father to come home.

In the afternoon, we slipped over to Frau Benz's house where she made sandwiches and tea. The street was full of soldiers. Several Jewish-owned homes were smoldering on our street. Looking out the window, I could see soldiers and work crews cleaning up glass and debris from the delicatessen, bakery, and meat market across the street were we did most of our shopping.

That night we sat huddled in a corner of Frau Benz's living room covered by a blanket. Each time the droning of a truck's engine or loud, hysterical voices intruded we trembled in silence.

The next morning, Frau Benz decided to go to the nearest police station and inquire about her husband and my father. After all, Herr Benz was German, and the secret police had no right to interfere with his activities. I wanted to go with her, but she thought it best that I go back to my house, lock the doors, close the shutters, and wait until she returned.

Walking into my house was like walking into a dark tunnel. I was in the dark but totally unaware of the darkness.

"Daddy, where are you? Why did you leave me?" I spoke to the quietness in the room. The sudden loud stomping sound of soldiers marching quickly diverted my focus and reality returned.

I closed the door and checked all the shutters to make sure they were secure. Then I sat by the window and thought about my father. He was all the family I had. I prayed to God that I wouldn't lose him. My prayer was interrupted by a loud rattling of the door. A voice bellowed:

"Ist niemand da"? (is anyone home). Once more the door rattled, and it sounded as if they were trying to batter it down. Then silence. Minutes later, the sound was repeated at Frau Benz's house.

I peeked through the shutter and saw soldiers everywhere, knocking on doors and running wildly through the neighborhood. I crawled under my bed and cried myself to sleep.

Later, I was awaken by a light rapping on my door and a soft voice calling to me.

"Hermann ... Hermann open the door. It's Frau Benz."

I opened the door, and she wrapped me in her arms.

"Are you all right?"

"Yes. Soldiers were here and also at your house."

"Yes I know. They are everywhere."

"What are they looking for?"

She hesitated to answer but changed her mind when she saw my frozen stare and furrowed brow.

"They are searching houses to find out who's living there. It's like ... well, a survey."

"What did you find out at the police station? Anything about my father and Herr Benz?"

"No. But the police are checking. I will be informed if they find anything. Now, I think it's best that you come over to my house. Get your clothing, and you will stay with me until we find out what happened."

We waited until all the soldiers had left our street, and under the cover of darkness, I moved my things over to Frau Benz's house. I was relaxed being with her, and I could sense she felt the same. I believe that deep down inside we both knew we would never see our loved ones again, and that solemn awareness hinged us closer together.

Frau Benz and I went to school the next day only to discover that most of the German boys had been taken away to special youth camps, and the school was closing for lack of students. Urged by the many guards surrounding the school, we returned home. But Frau Benz made the determination that I would continue my education.

Because Frau Benz and her husband were teachers, their home included an extensive library of educational material. She made a daily schedule of subjects I needed to study and critiqued me each evening on what I had learned. The most interesting subject, and the one I looked forward to each day, was music.

Frau Benz had a piano, violin, and cello in her home. She was an accomplished musician on each instrument and a patient, understanding teacher. Although I enjoyed listening to jazz records, and playing from sheet music my father had bought me, Frau Benz and I played mostly from classical composers. Our favorites were composers from Hamburg: Johannes Brahams—'Piano concerto No 1 in D minor'—Frau Benz alternated on violin and cello—and Felix Mendelssohn's 'A midsummers night dream,' and parts of his 'Italian and Scotch symphonies.'

As a protest, we refused to play music from Richard Strauss, although it was heard throughout the day on the radio, because he was closely affiliated with the Third Reich.

One day, as we happily played our favorite music a loud rattling sound shook the door.

"Hermann, go quickly to the basement. Be very quiet." Frau Benz said.

I tried to listen to the conversation as I stood behind the closed basement door, but the loud sounds from the street made it difficult. The room Frau Benz had given me in the basement was nice and comfortable, but I couldn't shake the sinking feeling that I might be in that basement for a long time.

Later, Frau Benz came down to the basement.

"That was a man from the police station. The police think they may have found my husband."

"And my father?" I asked with great hope and anticipation.

She looked at me and reached for my hands, like a mother about to give a polite scolding to her child. But Frau Benz's tone was warm and reassuring.

"He wasn't sure about your father. The man said a Professor Benz had been arrested along with his friends, and charged with treason."

"Treason? What is that?"

"Listen, dear. I feel that you and I are in for some bad times ahead, but regardless of what we find out, or what might happen in the future, we must have faith and hope. You understand?"

"Yes, I understand. But I still don't know what treason is."

"Its when a person does something terribly wrong against his country."

Immediately, I thought about the conversation I'd overheard between Herr Benz and my father. "Well, Karl, what can we do?"

"I don't know. Whatever we do we'll be risking our lives. But we need to do something."

I wanted to tell Frau Benz what I'd heard, but I was afraid it could be true—that they had tried to do something and were caught.

"I have permission to go to Berlin where these people are being held, to see if this man is really my husband."

"Can I go, too."

"Yes dear." She folded me in her arms. "We'll go together. There is, however, something else you need to know. The man from the police station wanted to know who was playing music with me." She pushed me gently away, and her soft brown eyes held me captive.

"I told him you were my servant. That you live in the basement, and you help me to care for the house since my husband's disappearance. He believed me and said it was okay. What do you think about what I did?"

"Okay, I guess. But what exactly does a servant do?"

"Oh, sweetheart, you're not my servant. You're more like the son I never had, and I love you dearly. Do you believe me?"

"Yes, and I love you too." She probably didn't realize it, but she was the mother I never had. Whatever she did or wanted to do was okay with me.

"Thank you, darling. Now, we're going to Berlin, and I want you to promise me that whatever we find out, you will be strong and brave, and the love and respect you have for your father, will never die. Promise?"

"I promise."

CHAPTER 6—QUESTIONS AND ANSWERS

Reading my grandfather's journal was an incredible educational experience. It was like living in two separate time periods. I was being inundated with knowledge and images that I probably would never have been aware of. I couldn't understand why very little, if anything at all, had been written about the Black Man's experience under Hitler's regime. I realized it was minuscule—comparing the Black Man's experience to that of Jews and Gypsies—but it *was* a harrowing occurrence and should have been recorded.

Reading about the horrors of *Kristallnacht* reminded me of the California riots. I saw people, live on TV, being snatched from cars and trucks—beaten, kicked, and left lying in the street. My inquisition was: what is the reward for such brutality? The neighborhoods being torched; who lived in those buildings, and benefited from local merchants? And when it was all over; who suffered the most? Perhaps the fundamental difference between the two riots was the explicitness. *Kristallnacht* was aimed explicitly at Jews. California riots were aimed at the "establishment." Nevertheless, when it was all over, it was people who suffered.

My reading hadn't advanced to the part where Grandpa was incarcerated in a concentration camp, and for me, there was no unbounded urgency in reaching that part of the journal.

My life was suddenly in a changing mode. A spontaneous sense of awareness became an integral part of my daily life. It was as if I were gradually being awakened from a long, dreary sleep. Consciously, I became more subjective about things that affected me as a young Black Man. In my past experiences, things that perhaps should've been placed under closer scrutiny, just flew by like a solitary leaf caught up in a raging windstorm. My only rationalization for my actions: I'd been so immersed in my music that I was sheltering under the false assumption that music would heal the soul and nothing else really mattered.

My first realization of real-world-living came during the interview with the school principal. Mr. Saberstein never once said what the school board or the parents wanted only what *he* wanted for *his* students. Because I was reading about a dictator who almost destroyed the world, I began to wonder what I should do, if anything, about Mr. Saberstein and his dictatorial attitude. I purposely avoided talking to Grandpa because he was visibly wounded when I carelessly threw Sigrid's name at him as if he knew all about her. I promised never to do that again, and in order to start at the beginning I needed to properly introduce Mr. Saberstein to my grandfather. I decided it would be the first thing on the agenda the next time we discussed the journal.

On this particular morning, Grandpa slept longer than usual.

Normally, his sleep routine was precise: in bed at 10:00 p.m. and up at 6:00 a.m. I noticed he was now sleeping later each day, and his physical appearance was deteriorating. His fingers for instance, once lean and nimble, were curling inward like a useless claw, and at times vibrated with uncontrolled silent taps against his palms. I knew he needed special care, but he'd made me promise him early on that I would never put him in a nursing home. I felt an urgent need to finish his journal because it seemed the only thing he cared about. He was reliving experiences that had been suppressed for too long, and I feared that once we finished, he would give up hope.

When he emerged from his bedroom, I was adding the finishing touches to his favorite breakfast: western omelet, toast, orange juice, and coffee.

"Sit down, Grandpa; breakfast is ready."

"Thanks, son, but I'm not too hungry. Coffee and toast will do fine."

"But, Grandpa, you're barely eating. You need to keep your strength."

"For what?" He said, and sipped his coffee.

I just let it go. I didn't want to get involved in a discussion about his illness.

"I read some more of your journal last night," I said casually.

"You did! How far did you get?" He leaned forward in his chair.

"I read the part where you returned home from the Olympic games and what happened afterward.

"And? Judging from the look on your face, you have questions."

His face was all lit up, dark eyes gleaming like polished rocks, and I knew that whatever I wanted to say about Mr. Saberstein could wait.

"It was interesting, Grandpa, and also emotional. Yes, I jotted down a few questions. Why did the Jewish teachers stop showing up for work? You didn't explain that?"

He poured himself another cup of coffee, and sat back in his chair. He looked so serene as he spoke.

"After Hitler came to power, he passed many laws against the Jewish people. One such law was to prohibit Jews from holding any position in the government. Realizing what was happening, many Jews began looking for a way out of Germany. They sensed that the abrupt wave of suppression was just the beginning of something horrible. They were given an option to leave Germany, and many did. The sudden exodus was widespread, creating a devastating void in the cultural stability of the country, and resulting in a severe shortage of professionals and white collar workers. Everyone felt the loss, but no one dared complain."

"You mentioned 'Germany's period of low esteem.' Was this caused by the exodus of Jews?"

"No. This was a totally different period. After World War I, Germany's economy sank to its lowest ebb. In order to punish Germany for its aggression during the war, the Allied Powers stripped Germany of all its major resources. All colonies were taken away and distributed to other countries. Heavy financial obligations forced banks into bankruptcy.

"More than half of the male population had been killed in the war. No jobs, more than six million people unemployed—It was a country that had been defeated at war and placed under strict sanctions. Its people had no future."

"After Hitler spoke at the Junior Olympics and the boys 'beamed' after he left. You said you 'beamed' too. But you felt nothing. What did you mean?"

"We were just boys attending an athletic competition to have fun. However, some of the boys were more excited about the prospect of Hitler's visit than winning at the games. I simply didn't share their enthusiasm. After he'd finished speaking and they applauded wildly, I applauded too, but I was just caught up in the joviality of the time. He meant absolutely nothing to me."

"Can you explain more about the youth groups? Were they like the Boy Scouts we have in America?"

"No! Absolutely not. They were not like American Boy Scouts. Hitler and his leaders were obsessed with physical training because it was closely related to military training. All children in school were required to play physically demanding games. Sports was mandatory for all university students. Many hours were devoted to the playing field, running track, marching, and handling light weapons. Finally, the Third Reich took over the sports movement and made it a priority of the state. All sports programs were coordinated and supervised down to the lowest level. Competitive sporting events were given highest priority. Advocates of the sports program admitted that it made all the male participants good material for the army.

"In the beginning, membership in the youth groups was not compulsory. But later, a decree was issued that *urged* all government workers to show their devotion by putting their sons in Hitler's youth groups to support the work of the Fuhrer.

"None of the boys in youth groups objected to being a member—they were honored. So, it didn't bother them when their curriculum included military sports. They were required to go twice a week and train on the assault courses that had been built on the campus of all schools. They participated in throwing wooden grenades, scaling walls, nets, and crossing imaginary chasms with ropes. It was all great fun. As the boys aged, new levels of attainments were established—some with strong military overtones: target and marching practice, which included shooting, forced marches, and aggressive forms of discussion. Other requirements were map-reading, knowledge of country, camouflage, and reporting information about enemy observations.

"The overall aim of the Nazi leaders was to produce and shape from the youth groups a constant stream of potential recruits who could be converted into full-scale soldiers with the minimum of time and training."

"Did you ever find out why the black students left school?"

"Yes. There were two groups of Africans or <u>Mohrens</u> in Germany during that time.

One group were descendants of slaves, like my father, who came to Germany during the late 1800s and integrated into German society. Most were professionals and considered themselves citizens of Germany. Some, along with Jewish citizens, participated in World War I in support of Germany. The second group were Africans who were victims of colonization by Germany.

As I said earlier, Germany changed its attitude in dealing with its African colonies and began treating them as human beings. This form of treatment impressed members of the African colonies, and when these colonies were dissolved at the end of the war, many felt they were a part of Germany and escaped to Germany where they began a new life. But in 1933, when Hitler became Chancellor, and in 1935, when the Nuremberg citizenship laws were enacted, a red flag was raised: 'A citizen of the Reich is only that subject who is of German or kindred blood.' Some returned to Africa, others migrated to other parts of the world. Men like my father, ignored the Nuremberg laws and continued their work. They were proud German citizens and felt the laws could not deprive them of their lawful citizenship."

"What is a 'Rhineland Bastard'? Did you ever find out why the soldiers called you that?"

"Rhineland Bastard, was a name given to children born of a relationship between German women and African soldiers. You might remember that after World War II, children born under similar situations with Black American soldiers as fathers were called 'Brown Babies.'

"After World War I, the Allies established a demilitarized zone as a buffer between Germany and Western Europe. African soldiers from French colonies were stationed in the Rhineland to patrol the demilitarized zone, and fraternization occurred. Ironically, these children were among the first to be sterilized."

"What was the assassination that triggered the *Kristallnacht* riots?"

"Actually, it was an attempted assassination that initially triggered the riots. The victim died sometime after the riots had ended.

"It all started with the deep-seated hate and rage of a young Jewish man born in Germany, but whose parents were born in Poland. The Nuremberg laws on citizenship excluded him and his family as citizens of Germany. As a matter of fact, all Jews were excluded from citizenship: 'A Jew cannot be a citizen of the Reich. He cannot exercise the right to vote; he cannot occupy public office.' But, he really went over the edge while he was in Paris visiting relatives who had escaped from Germany. The young man saw that Hitler's sweep to get rid of Jews had included his hometown where complete Jewish neighborhoods were cleared and the occupants taken and dumped on Poland's soil. The young man wanted revenge; he wanted to kill someone in the German hierarchy to bring worldwide attention to what was going on in Germany. The German Embassy in Paris was his best bet. But instead of shooting the Ambassador, he shot a lowly secretary.

"Nevertheless, it was an insult on the Third Reich. What followed was the release of another vindictive rage built up by the Nazi regime against Jews. It was supposed to have been a 'controlled rage.' That is to say, certain procedures were established so as not to expose the latent barbarism of the Third

Reich. But communications filtering down didn't reach the proper authorities who were supposed to be in control. For instance, there were messages that allowed destruction of Jewish property, but no abuse was to come to the Jewish population. Most of those messages were not received, or if received, ignored. So the *Pogroms* began and will remain in history as the world's worst riot."

My grandfather became visibly animated as he answered my questions. He was feeding off the questions as if they were some miracle drug that was going to cure his illness. It was good to see him so alive, but I knew it had to end. I thought that maybe introducing my problem with Mr. Saberstein would keep him going.

"Grandpa, I don't have anymore questions about the journal now. I will read more tonight, and tomorrow we'll have some more discussions. You have made everything understandably clear. I do, however, have some questions about a particular problem I might face when I start teaching." There was a curious glow in his eyes as he leaned forward.

"What kind of problem, son?"

"During my interview, the principal lectured me on the type of music *he* wanted taught in *his* school. He said that all music outside of classical music is 'bastard music.'"

"And where exactly do you see the problem?"

"It's a potential problem. But I feel very strongly that it could easily become a real problem because he alone is setting the standards for the kids going to school—not the school board, not the Parent-Teachers Association. I just think it's wrong."

"What grade level will you be teaching?"

"Middle and high school. Most of these kids play in the school band, which means they have advanced through the rudiments of music. I know that their interest extends beyond Bach and Beethoven. I'm supposed to sign a contract that prohibits the introduction of blues, jazz, and other bastard music into the school's music program."

My grandfather sat quiet for a moment. Then he looked at me and said, "What happened when you were in middle and high school? What music did you, or were you, allowed to play?"

"As you know, you kept my interest in classical until I could read music, understood harmony, melody, rhythm, and composition, Then I was allowed to experiment. At school, my music teacher/bandmaster was very liberal with those of us who wanted to play various types of music. These kids at Mr. Saberstein's school are being deprived of the opportunity to learn about other types of music, and that is wrong."

"Why do you think it's wrong for adults to impose their will on children?"

"Because the learning process is a process of choice. Grandpa, you could not have made me play jazz, blues, or any of the other music I liked, if I had not wanted to play. I wanted to <u>learn</u>. To restrict these kids to only one type of music is to destroy their potential for growth in music. They must enjoy what they are doing. Am I being too sensitive about this, Grandpa?"

"No. But that is the uniqueness of Black people in America today—to spot the slightest and most perceptive traces of injustice. It was a new experience for me when I first arrived in America, and it took me some time to get used to it. Even New York City had its systems of injustice against certain ethnic groups. I found it on the job, in housing, and in the schools. Today, things are better, but you can still find isolated incidents. Hopefully, they are quickly challenged."

"Do you think Mr. Saberstein is one of those isolated cases? You know, Grandpa, since I've been reading your journal, I don't equate slavery with injustice. Granted, there is a lot of injustice in this world, but Hitler, in my mind, was the absolute dictator of injustice. He tried to impose his will of injustice not only on one race but several races of people. I'm wondering if he started out slowly like Mr. Saberstein?"

"Good point, son. As a matter of fact, it took Hitler many years to perfect his system of racial hatred. And if someone had been more perceptive in the early days, maybe our history books would read differently."

CHAPTER 7—THE PRISONER

Frau Benz and I rode the train from Hamburg to Berlin, hoping to find out what had happened to her husband and my father. I sat upright in my seat, my head pressed firmly against the headrest. The polished fabric covering my seat generated a familiar smell—antiseptic, like the mats in my gymnastic class. As the train whizzed past farms and villages, I could see fog rising slowly from the ground, like smoke from a smoldering fire. Fall was about to invade Germany.

It was my second time on a train other than the streetcars I rode to school. My first time was the trip back from Berlin after the Olympics. That was a sad trip because I had been forced to watch as Hitler publicly embarrassed Jessie Owens, my hero and a member of my race. I was hoping this trip would be more positive—that we would find Herr Benz and my father. The police in Berlin had said they were holding a Professor Benz, along with his friends. They had been arrested and charged with treason for trying to send inflammatory messages to the foreign press about alleged unlawful arrests and brutal beatings of Jews and others during *Kristallnacht.*

I glanced at Frau Benz sitting next to me. Her long brown coat, with its furry collar, was buttoned up to her neck. Her waist-length brown hair had been wrapped neatly into a soft ball behind her head and covered with a bowl-like hat.

On this day she was especially beautiful, although my gaze was continually drawn to the unnatural color of her lips. I'd never seen her wear lipstick before, and her pallid complexion emphasized the stark pink color. When she saw me staring, she reached and grabbed my hand.

We sat in silence, pretending not to notice people who, after seeing a respectable looking German woman holding hands with a black boy, decided to sit in another coach. My thoughts were on my father, and I really didn't care about anyone else. But Frau Benz was visibly upset, and when she looked at me I could see the water level rising in her eyes as the train eased into the station.

Berlin was not the same sonorous and festive city I'd seen when we visited the Olympics. No civilians walked on the streets, but workers scurried like ants rebuilding, repairing, and removing debris from burned-out buildings apparently damaged from Kristallnacht.

When the taxi pulled up to the police station, my body felt glued to my seat. It was like a paralyzing premonition signaling that something was terribly wrong. Then I heard Frau Benz's voice.

"Come on, Hermann. It's okay."

Suddenly I was rushing up the steps to the entrance. Inside, was an arresting scene. Old and young civilians with blank stares and hungry, distraught looks, moved with slow and heavy gaits in a straight line toward the rear of the station, while young guards with rifles in hand yelled, pushed, and prodded them along.

What I didn't know then was they were on their way to concentration camps and possible death.

"Yes, this is my husband." Frau Benz seized the photograph from the policeman behind the high desk, and I saw the blood drain from her face, leaving it pallid. "Good Lord, what ... what have you done to my husband?" Her voice, when she spoke, was ghastly, as if she were choking back a scream.

"Your husband is a traitor." The policeman retorted. "We do not tolerate treason in the Third Reich."

"Just...let me see my husband." Frau Benz was struggling to compose herself. I wanted to get a look at the picture, but the officer snatched it away. "How about a Professor Hoffmann? He is the father of this young man. He was with my husband the night he disappeared... ."

The policeman eyed me as if he were surveying a dead body, then whispered to another policeman who motioned for me to follow him. I looked apprehensively at Frau Benz.

"Go ahead, Hermann. We'll meet here after you've seen your father."

I followed the officer through the station house, past cells bulging with people. Wailing sounds of desperation leaped out for help; hands with extended fingers stretched through the bars in a feeble attempt to touch me. I was only thirteen, but I felt at least twenty walking behind that officer. But when I descended into the semi-dark basement, the thirteen-year-old mentality returned, paired with fear. I hesitated, feeling the sudden fleetness of my heartbeat, but the policeman waved me on.

At the bottom of the stairs was a long, narrow hallway with cell blocks on both sides. One naked light bulb, hanging in the center of the room above the hallway, cast dim shadows. As I walked down the hallway, the sound of my footsteps echoed like beats of muted tom toms. I couldn't see any visible signs of life behind those bars, but the harsh sound of groans and movement crowded my ears as I passed each cell. Suddenly, like a violent gust of hot air, the putrid smell of human waste filtered through my nostrils, triggering my stomach. Swiftly covering my nose and mouth to quell the overwhelming desire to vomit, I followed the policemen closely until he stopped. He pointed to a darken cell and I approached it cautiously, afraid to look inside.

"*Zehn minuten*" (ten minutes), he said as he walked away.

I peered into the dark cell, my gaze scanning the eerie blackness. "Dad! Are you in there?" I waited, still fighting the eruptive surging in my stomach. I heard someone breathing heavily. "Dad! This is Hermann. Is that you?" Then I heard the sound I had been waiting to hear.

"Hermann?" The voice was broken and barely audible, but I recognized the subtle inflections.

"Yes, Dad. It's Hermann. Can you see me? I'm over here." I slapped the iron bars repeatedly with the palm of my hand, hoping he could follow the sound in the semi-darkness. My heart was racing, and suddenly I wanted to cry out with joy. I have found my father! But I waited. Then I heard the scratching sound of movement, as if someone was dragging a cardboard box over the naked floor.

Through shadows of the overhead light, I saw him sliding slowly toward me. My first moment of terror came when his hand, covered with tattered and soiled white bandages, grasped the bars next to me. He pulled himself closer, and I fought to stifle a scream. It wasn't my father!

"Hermann?" He whispered, and it was my father.

"Dad? Are you all right?" I was numb. An abrupt flow of algid air had surrounded me, slowly freezing my body. I kneeled down as his shoulder rested gingerly against the bars. His head was covered with blood-soaked bandages; his face disfigured with cuts and bruises. "What happened, Dad? Did they beat you?"

"Yes, son." His voice was a wheeze, and I had to lean closer to hear him. "Don't worry about me. How are you?"

"I'm okay. The schools are closed, but I'm living with Frau Benz."

"That's good. You stay with her. She will take good care of you until I come home. Now there is something I want you to do for me. Listen closely." He reached for my hand and held it tightly. "Disregard the bad things you may have heard, or read about me. They're not true. All we did was try to help change the horrible times we're going through. They beat us to make us confess, but we didn't. There will be a trial soon, but I have no great expectations of the outcome."

"But father, you're hurt. Can't they at least put you in a hospital?"

"Look, son. These are evil people. It's like a wave of madness has spread swiftly over this country, inflicting everyone. There is nothing we can do but try to stay alive, hope, and pray this nightmare will soon be over. Don't you try anything that will provoke them. Go quietly about your business, and do not say anything publicly against what is going on. If you do, they will find you and silence you. Promise me that if I don't come home soon, you'll continue studying your music and grow into the man I know you can become. If you ever have a chance to leave this God-forsaken country, grab it. Anywhere in the world is better than here."

"Raus!" The voice of a policeman called to me. It was time to go.

"You must go now, son," my father said.

"No!" I screamed. The same rage I felt at the Olympic stadium that day when Hitler snubbed Jessie Owens was seething inside my young body, only this time it was a powder keg with the fuse burning. I will not leave until you get a doctor for my father." The policeman approached me slowly. He had no weapon, and hurriedly in the back of my mind, I was trying to figure out what to do next. In my gymnastic classes we'd practiced self defense movements against each other, but this was real. I had decided on the proper protective maneuver when my father yanked my hand.

"Hermann, please go. There is nothing good you can do here. He released my hand and I turned to walk away. But I whirled when the policeman spoke again.

"*Raus*! Neger Bastard, *Raus*!"

It was the second time I'd heard the word *bastard* spoken, but it was the harsh enmity in the tone of his voice, and the way he looked at me when he said those words, that made my body react with all its gymnastic ability. I lunged into his chest with both feet, knocking him backward to the floor. His voice rose in a plea for help as I rushed toward him. He was struggling to get to his feet when I grabbed his shoulder and spun him over. Angry voices chanted from the cells: "Kill him, kill him." But among those imposing voices was the unmistakable sound of my father's voice pleading to me, "Hermann, stop. Please stop." I looked at the policeman. His eyelids were elevated and frozen. His mouth gaped, and his lips quivered. He was young—maybe a few years older than me. We stared at each other, and for one ambivalent moment, I believe we both realized that we were just young boys caught up in a period of hostility, hate, and violence. Suddenly, several arms were about me, wrestling me to the floor. Hearing my father's voice calling my name, I didn't know whether he could see them carrying me up the stairs like a sack of potatoes, but the last thing I heard before the steel door slammed shut behind us was my name in a chilling scream that could possibly have been my father's last breath.

Once upstairs the policemen dropped me to the floor. Then they made me stand up while each officer took turn kicking my butt through the station and out the door.

The burning ache on my butt wasn't so apparent until the door was closed behind me. Then, I kneeled down on the damp steps and cried until Frau Benz came out.

The mood on the train going back to Hamburg was the same somber disposition we had going to Berlin, only this time we knew the harsh reality of our situation. Even though Herr Benz and my father were going to trial, we knew the odds were very high they would be convicted. On the other hand, if they were not convicted, they would never be released from jail. Surprisingly, there were no tears. We simply looked at each other with sad admittance of the hopelessness of our situation and held hands until the train stopped in Hamburg. The ache on my butt from the policemen's boots made it difficult to walk straight as we departed the train.

Our neighborhood in Wilhelmsburg was rapidly reestablishing itself. The delicatessen, bakery, and other shops wrecked during the "Night of Broken Glass" were reopening with new owners and unfamiliar faces.

Our house was still closed. Sometimes I would sneak in at night to check if anyone had broken in or disturbed our possessions. I had no idea what I was going to do about the house. It was in my father's name, and I could only wait for the outcome of the trial. My whole life was ingrained in that house. It was my birthplace; the place where my mother died bringing me into the world. For me, it was a great monument of everything good in the world.

The neighborhood was also showing signs of returning to normalcy. No soldiers on the streets; a few sailors walked about. Otherwise, all semblance of chaos had disappeared.

This tranquil period was due largely to Hitler's army moving away in search of more important conquests. He had taken over Austria without any resistance, and the supporters of the Third Reich were rejoicing in what they perceived as a true statement: "*Deutschland Uber Alles*" (Germany Over Everyone).

Frau Benz managed to find a new teaching position at a different school. She left early each morning while I was sleeping and returned in the afternoon for my music lessons. During the day, I tried to keep occupied with my studies and taking short walks, hoping to find some of my old school friends. But they were all gone. My friends were mysteriously missing. When I ventured to some of their homes to inquire about them, doors would slam violently in my face, or angry and vicious words like the ones used by the policeman, would leap out at me like flames from the mouth of an angry dragon. When I walked away, the swift movement of curtains at each window was evidence someone was watching. When meeting people on the street, I could predict they would cross over or walk out in the middle of the street rather than meet me. It was strange and totally bewildering, because I had walked the same streets with my father without incident. They were the same streets where my friends and I played soccer together many warm and muggy summer afternoons. Now the streets were deserted. I felt lost—like I was the only child left in the world.

My music was all I had left to play with, and I played it daily with all the anger and intensity in me. So many times I thought if I was a man I could do something to effect a change. But thinking about my father's fruitless efforts left me without an answer or motivation.

One day, at the end of my music lessons, Frau Benz spoke suddenly. Her voice was impassive—not the same warm voice that corrected me when I strayed in my chord progression. This voice had a stark urgency that demanded my attention.

"Hermann, I think we should leave here. It's not safe anymore."

"Why? What's the problem?" I could see the deep lines of concern in the tiny wrinkles around the corners of her mouth. I realized that those wrinkles, and others I hadn't noticed before, had boldly appeared and were squeezing her face. Her deep, hazel eyes that were soothing when I was upset avoided me. She turned her back, threading her fingers slowly through her long chestnut hair.

"Oh, my God." She sighed.

"What's wrong, Frau Benz?" She turned abruptly and those hypnotic eyes locked into mine.

"People are talking!" she said, her hands folded sternly across her breast as if she were giving a confession. "You are not a little boy anymore. You're a handsome young man, and ... and people don't believe me anymore when I tell them you are my servant. I'm just afraid for both of us. You understand?"

"Yes, I understand." I lied. "But where can we go? And what about our houses?"

"I have a brother who lives on a farm just outside the city. I've already talked to him and he understands what is going on and has invited us to stay with him on his farm until things get better. Our homes will be okay. There won't be anymore Kristallnachts. When the trial is over, we can decide what to do. In the meantime, you can help my brother on the farm and I will continue to teach. Everything will be fine. What do you think?"

One of the reasons I had so much admiration for Frau Benz was because of her insistence of my opinion on things that affected me. It made me feel important, and even though I always agreed with her, it was the thought that mattered.

"Okay, I guess." I said, and her face lit up, pushing back the tiny wrinkles. "But, I don't know anything about working on a farm."

"Don't worry, dear. Wolfgang will teach you." She gave a jovial laugh that made me happy.

I had an unshakable trust in Frau Benz. Also, I felt responsible for her. She was very pretty, and each time she hugged and kissed me, the feelings I experienced were not the feelings a son should have for his mother.

CHAPTER 8—THE EXECUTION

My grandfather's sleep patterns were changing drastically. Some nights were sleepless, and he'd sleep all day, or half the night was sleepless, and he'd sleep until midday. This dramatic change was interfering with our relationship. I couldn't prepare his breakfast not knowing when he would awake. Lunch was always a wild guess, and sometimes we had dinner together. I missed our long, animated conversations, and the house was becoming more like the quietness of a library.

I was deeply concerned and decided to visit Doctor Simon who had diagnosed my grandfather for symptoms of Alzheimer's disease. As we talked, I had a chilling feeling that Doctor Simon was trying to prepare me for my grandfather's demise.

"We don't know how long your grandfather has been ill," he said. "He came to us about middle-stage and we can only guess how long it will be before the final stage kicks in," he said, avoiding my prying eyes.

"Dr. Simon, I'm not concerned about how long my grandfather has to live. What I am concerned about is making him comfortable while he is alive. And in order to do that, I must know more about Alzheimer's disease."

"Are you planning to become his sole caregiver?" He stared at me. I assumed he was talking about me being a nurse or something, so in order not to sound stupid, I uttered the first thing that came off my brain.

"If that's what it takes."

He continued staring at my face; his gaze searching to make contact. I refused to look at him. I guess he knew that I was just a confused young man who knew absolutely nothing about taking care of a seriously ill person.

"Look!" He walked behind his desk that was piled high with colorful file folders. "I admire your courage, but I'm afraid you haven't the slightest clue as to what you're getting into. These are cases of Alzheimer's patients we have here in the hospital."

He pointed to the stack of files. "There are so many cases that we had to create a special Alzheimer's unit to handle the overload. More than six million Americans are afflicted, and until we find a cure, our caseload will continue to swell. We don't have any space left. Every hospital in the United States has the same problem. We are thankful that about seventy percent of all Alzheimer's patients are cared for in the home by family and friends, but when the patients reach a certain stage of progression, it's best if they are cared for in a professional setting." He looked at me to see what effect his message was having on me.

"Alzheimer's disease," he continued, "is a progressive, degenerative disease of the brain in which the brain cells die and are not replaced. You see, the brain tells the body what to do: to stand up, to walk, to swallow, and to breathe. When this function stops, the patient will die.

"Caring for an Alzheimer's patient is a challenging and emotional task. It's an emotional roller coaster ride in which the caregiver is encouraged to find some means of relieving their own stress to avoid serious depression. The caregiver must meet and overcome these threatening challenges. What do you think, so far?"

I didn't know what to think. I felt he was testing me, and I resented that. When I didn't answer, he spoke again.

"My advice to you is stop by the reception desk on your way out, and get all the published material you can find on Alzheimer's disease. Read it. Try to understand as much as you can, and when you have questions, stop by and see me. It's a good thing what you're attempting to do. I wish more young people had the courage to make the same sacrifice you're planning."

"I'm the only family he has. What am I suppose to do... just throw him away... put him in a nursing home and let him die of loneliness?"

He stared at me again. I think he was satisfied that he'd ruffled me and tapped into my emotional pool.

"You have no other help? Perhaps it's best if we put him on the waiting list."

"No!" My voice rose, and my emotional pool threatened to overflow. "He made me promise I wouldn't put him in a nursing home, and I have every intention of keeping that promise."

"You may not have a choice. You see, the rate of progression is unpredictable. One day he may appear fine, and the following day could be a horror scene. You must be prepared to handle it."

Suddenly, I was quiet. I knew the doctor was right. But I just had to keep Grandpa home. We had so much to do: We had to finish the journal together, and at home was the proper place to do that. He needed to completely relive his time and experiences during Hitler's regime—especially his time in the concentration camp. He had to put a definitive closure to all of it. It pained me to even think that a member of may family had been in a concentration camp. Even though there were no visible physical scars, I could only imagine what mental agony he must have endured. I looked at the doctor who had a blank, impatient stare as if to say, "your time is up."

"Doctor," I spoke abruptly, "my grandfather went through some difficult times during the war and is haunted by the memories. Will this compound his illness?"

His bland expression almost produced a smile. I felt he approved of the question. Maybe it was the first intelligent remark I'd made during my visit.

"No," he said, his hands in motion as if giving a lecture. "Alzheimer's disease, over a period of time, will impair or completely wipe out all memory, thinking, and past behavior. It becomes the 'Grim Reaper,' if you will, of its victims."

Once again I was speechless. I felt I was struggling against time. All my grandfather wanted was to tell his story—to admit freely and openly what had happened to him under Hitler's regime. Perhaps he thought he was the only one left to tell the story.

How many Black Men died at that special camp, and why were they there? The answers were in the pages of his journal.

Many times I had a pressing urge to flip through the pages and find out all the details of his actual time in that concentration camp, but I knew he wouldn't forgive me for getting ahead of the story.

"Is there anything else," the doctor was leading me toward the door, his gaze searching my face.

"No." I was so involved in my thoughts, I'd forgotten the last thing we'd discussed.

"If your grandfather shows any signs of being emaciated, incontinent, or immobile, you *must* commit him to a nursing home. You understand?" He reached for my hand. His shake was firm and felt sincere.

I nodded, but I couldn't see myself breaking my promise to Grandpa. He was my responsibility, and we would get through this horrible ordeal together.

Returning home, I was filled with anxiety from my conversation with Doctor Simon. Some of the words, *emaciated* and *incontinent*, were not in my active vocabulary, so I'd planned to look them up.

"Grandpa!" I called, dropping the daily mail on the coffee table. There was no answer. I knew he was home, so I called again and walked through the living room toward his bedroom. I heard a distinct sound, and was relieved because it was water running in the bathroom. "Grandpa!" I called again. "Are you in there"? I stood before the bathroom door.

"Yes," was the reply, "come on in." I smiled and heaved a sigh of relief. But it quickly disappeared when I opened the door. Grandpa was seated in the bathtub soaping himself with a bath towel. He smiled at me. My hand gripped the door knob. Grandpa was wearing his pajamas. I gave an abbreviated wave, closed the door, walked slowly back into the living room, and started mechanically sorting the pile of mail. Consciously, I had just witnessed what doctor Simon was trying to get me to see. Subconsciously, I ignored it as I sifted through the pile of advertisers' long-shots and found a letter from Sigrid.

I loved her handwriting. I always watched her in class. The left hand would curve intimately over the paper as if she were going to caress it, then the pen she held so precariously printed each letter of the alphabet so neatly that it looked as if it had been printed by machine.

She was coming to New York, the letter read. Her father had been successful in getting her an audition with the New York Symphony Orchestra and the Boston Symphony Orchestra. They would be arriving in a few weeks. She wanted me to meet her parents, and hopefully, she could meet mine.

Sigrid and I were dear friends, but I felt deflated that she, so many thousand of miles away, could get an audition in New York while I lived one hour from Manhattan and was only looking forward to teaching a bunch of middle school kids. Sure, she was talented, but so was I. My feeling was that equally talented people should have an equal chance at success. At least that was my interpretation of the Equal Rights Amendment.

Then, I realized that the impeding real-world difference between success and failure in our society, is "who you know."

Obviously, her father had a lot of influence in the upper levels of society. I knew it wasn't fair, but I also knew that my day would come.

I didn't know whether I wanted to meet her family, nor was I overly happy having them meet Grandpa. But later, when I mentioned it to him, he was delighted.

"This is great! I've long wanted to talk to someone from the new generation of Germans, especially the *Nach Krieg Kind* (after the war babies), to explore their feelings and attitudes about what happened during the war."

I didn't think it was a good idea. I was fearful that confronting the people who tried to kill him might have an adverse effect on his illness. But he displayed no visible animosity, and whatever made him happy, I was willing to do. Besides, I was curious to find out their reaction once they learned Grandpa had been in a concentration camp.

That night, as I reached for the journal, I had to once again restrain myself from looking at the ending—the concentration camp. I felt guilty, like an abused child who expects punishment for any impure thought.

Frau Benz and I rode a train and a bus to her brother's home. It was located in a strictly agricultural community just outside of Hamburg. Quaint houses sat uniformly along the road that separated them from the Elbe River. Each house exhibited its own unique color scheme. They were half-timbered houses, with A-frame fronts and colorful wooden slats that zigzagged across them, like the tedious strokes of an artist who'd slashed paint across his canvas in a wavering moment of disgust.

Heavy wooden shutters lay open, like lapels of a fancy suit, exposing the plate-glass windows and white frilly curtains. Flower boxes, with assorted blooming flowers, adorned each window and bordered front doors.

Each lawn sprouted the greenest grass I'd ever seen and was edged with flowers, shrubs or plants. The site was a beautiful rainbow collection of homes.

Beyond the fronts were the tools of farming: barns, animals, wagons, tractors, and fields that extended outward in measured plots.

Wolfgang greeted me with a hug so strong that I thought I'd suffocate from his massive strength and body odor. He looked like a Samari wrestler minus the voluminous waistline.

"Hilda has told me so much about you. Now, we're finally going to be friends," he said, flashing a wide smile revealing teeth that desperately needed to become friendly with a toothbrush. "We'll be a family." He looked to his sister.

Frau Benz, who's first name I had just learned was "Hilda," began shedding happy tears. She hugged her brother, and soon we were a trio hugging and laughing with happiness.

Wolfgang had prepared food for us—enough for ten people. But as we sat down and I watched him eat, I realized it was undoubtedly just a regular meal for him.

We talked briefly about the war. Hitler's army had successfully invaded Poland, Norway, and Denmark. The port of

Hamburg was very active in support of the war. It was the shipping hub of Germany and warships were constantly in and out with troops and supplies. When France was attacked, the war was suddenly closer to home. Rationing of almost everything became a way of life. Wolfgang and other farmers were required to provide most of their fruits, vegetables, meat, and dairy products to support the war.

Wolfgang had constructed a building behind his farmhouse to prepare and store his fruits and vegetables for market. But since he'd talked to his sister, he cleaned it out and prepared it for us.

It was a cinder-block building with several small rooms designed as storage rooms to segregate fruits and vegetables, but no indoor plumbing. As a matter of fact, there was no indoor plumbing in Wolfgang's house either. Water was pumped from a well in the backyard, and the toilet was a small house near the barnyard. Two mattresses had been placed in separate rooms with sheets, pillows, and feather quilts piled on top.

One round stove, with a smoke pipe that curved upwards and out the nearest wall, was the only source of heat.

The situation was bleak, but we decided it would do until the trial was over and we made a final decision on what to do. We returned to our houses with Wolfgang and gathered clothes, and other necessities to sustain us for what we felt would only be a short time.

One night several weeks later, after a grand meal prepared by Frau Benz, we sat drinking beer and wine deep into the night. Wolfgang fell asleep, and quietly we sneaked out the back door under the thunderous sound of his snoring.

It was a night I'll never forget. Blissfully, I entered into manhood. I was awkward, but she was patient. She guided me expertly along the sensual path of lovemaking. I responded with profound warmth, passion, and gratitude to the woman I once thought of as my mother. But from that night onward, she would be my lover.

Wolfgang's farm was primarily a dairy farm, but he had cherry and apple trees, grew potatoes, tomatoes, and cabbage. Each farmer worked equal acreage of land, but each farm had a diversity in what they produced. Collectively, they were a giant produce market that provided the urban towns with fresh milk and produce daily.

My first day as a farmer came when Wolfgang burst into our cabin and discovered his sister and me on the same mattress. He completely ignored the awkward situation and continued yelling.

"Lets go, Hermann! Time to work."

It was totally dark as I stumbled behind him, trying to finish dressing, on the way to the barn. He carried a lantern that swung backward and forward with his long strides. The dim glow highlighted only his yellow rubber boots squeezing through the soggy, straw-covered floor of the barn.

"Every morning, we must get the milk before the cows wakes up," Wolfgang said with a deep laugh, "because when they wake up they can be very, very mean."

The first few days as a farmer left me totally exhausted. At night, as much as I loved the new game called sex, I would lay hushed with aching muscles and fall asleep.

From the wee hours of the morning untill dusk, Wolfgang and I worked, stopping several times during the day to eat and drink. My most annoying adjustment to farming was learning how to milk the five cows. I felt there was a collective conspiracy against me. Wolfgang could sit down humming a tune, tug gently on the milk bags, and milk would stream down into the pail. But as soon as I sat down, all milk faucets were unexpectedly turned off. Wolfgang tried to soothe my dilemma by explaining how a cow and a woman share the same characteristics.

"A woman won't give her love to just anyone. It must be someone she has a feeling for," he said. "Cows are the same. Now you must make them like you."

"How?" I asked. It sounded like a stupid idea, but I decided to play along.

"You must feed them, give them water, pamper them, and even sing to them."

So, a great deal of my time was exhausted courting the cows. I found myself enjoying the one-sided conversations, and at times I caught the curious eyes of the cows watching me. Then it all paid off. One morning, when I tried getting milk, all faucets were fully open, and milk flowed like the beginning of a rainstorm.

We had a rigid routine; we woke up before daylight, and while Hilda (I had dropped the formal Frau Benz) prepared breakfast in Wolfgang's kitchen, he and I gathered pails of milk, which we sat out by the road in large containers for the collective milk wagon to pickup. Then, we went in to breakfast while Hilda prepared for work teaching.

Working on the farm was a wonderful experience, and my body was getting hard and muscle-bound from the manual labor. My energy level was exceedingly high and I was happy. I had gotten over my past tragedies, except for the trial, and I didn't want to think past that. The only thing I really missed was the piano in Hilda's house. We'd brought the violin and cello to the farm, and on weekends we made beautiful music, alternating on the instruments. Sometimes my fingers would get hard, cracked, and swollen from farm work, making it impossible to feel the delicate strings on the instruments. I had serious doubts whether I'd ever get the sensitivity back in my fingers.

Several times, when Hilda and I revisited our homes to see if anything had been stolen or damaged, I had tried to play the piano, but my fingers wouldn't respond to the chords I wanted to play. I often got up angrily and left. At night, Hilda soaked my fingers in warm water with an oily solution. Then she bought some gloves for me to use when I worked in those areas that could damage my hands.

We'd lived on the farm for about four months when our serene life collapsed.

One day, Hilda rushed home from work with tears spilling over her cheeks. She held up a local newspaper with bold headlines:

"TRAITORS OF THE FATHERLAND EXECUTED"

The article listed the towns, names, and addresses of those executed. The names listed under the town of Wilhelmsburg made us freeze with fear. My father and Herr Benz were the two names listed. The article urged the people in Wilhelmsburg to "rise up and chase the families and friends of those traitors of the Fatherland into the Elbe River."

I think we knew all along that we wouldn't ever see our loved ones again, but we never anticipated the kind of backlash the newspaper was proposing. Hilda was the first to break the terrifying silence.

"Oh, my God!" Her voice bordered on hysteria. "Our houses, we need to get everything out, quickly."

I was having the same thoughts, and we both turned to face Wolfgang.

"Wait here. I'll be back." He turned, and his huge body hustled out the door.

Hilda and I embraced, holding each other so close we could feel the pounding of each other's heartbeat. We weren't thinking so much of our safety as we were of our personal belongings. They were the memorabilia of our lives—our only connection with our past.

We were still cloaked in embrace when Wolfgang returned.

"Come on!" he yelled.

We dashed outside to help Wolfgang hook up an empty trailer that he used for hauling produce to market to his tractor.

"Get in!" Wolfgang bellowed while the tractor moved slowly forward, "We're going to move your things now." His voice resonated with solace and we climbed in, feeling extremely fortunate that we had someone like Wolfgang who could think rationally. When we entered the roadway that passed through the village, other tractors pulling empty trailers joined us. Suddenly, we had a convoy of tractors.

Hilda and I sat apart in the trailer, each thinking individual thoughts. I wondered how my father was executed. Remembering the condition he was in when last I saw him, he could've died before the trial was completed. But I would never know, and that ambiguous feeling would haunt me for the rest of my life.

I didn't know how long we'd been on the road, when the tractor slowed and stopped. We sat up and looked up front at Wolfgang. He was pointing ahead. It was then I saw circles of white smoke billowing upward toward the sky. I thought immediately of what I had seen the morning after *Kristallnacht*, when the synagogue and Jewish homes were burned. I leaped out of the trailer and ran toward the smoke. My mouth flew open and screaming sounds gushed from my throat. Whatever I was saying wasn't very articulate, but I felt like Jessie Owens as my legs propelled me onward. When I reached the entrance to the street where our houses were located, I stopped. A mob of people, yelling and screaming, were grouped around our two houses hurling containers of liquid fuel onto the structures as the flames soared. The loud, fanatical cheering and chanting clouded my hearing, but as I stood helplessly in the street I could feel the hairs on my legs being ignited and burning slowly up my body. Then, like the explosion of a blowtorch aimed directly at me, all hairs on my body were in flame. Feeling the sweltering heat devouring me, I turned sharply and panic propelled me back toward the tractor. The searing pain was hot and unbearable. I wanted to scream, but my throat was parched and dry. I continued running until I saw Wolfgang's outstretched arms, like a house in the middle of the street with its doors open. I ran inside and felt the warmth of his mammoth arms. My body was instantly cooled, and his soft voice in my ear chased away the vicious chanting of the mob.

"It's okay, Hermann. Everything will be okay." He picked me up and carried me, like a baby, to the trailer.

I heard him but I didn't respond because it wasn't 'OKAY!' My life—my heritage, was being burned to ashes in a town my father loved. He once told me that he and my mother bought the house in Wilhelmsburg because, "Wilhelmsburg is a workers city. A city where white and blue collar workers live side by side. The backbone of Hamburg. A city where Jews, Catholic, and Christians live and worship in an atmosphere of respect and tolerance. A city where neighbors can leave their doors open, and no one will enter unless invited."

I wanted to scoff at the statement about good neighbors. Most of that mob ringing around our house as it burned were our neighbors. What happened to his dream city?

The town of Wilhemsburg seemed to have changed into a jungle where neighbors had suddenly become predators at the whims of the government. A neighborhood where survival meant the purity of blood, fair skin, blue eyes, and the cunnings of a tiger.

Pain and anger obscured the reality of my non-existence. All the documentations of my being had been in my home—birth certificate, citizenship—my very scrolls of existence. I was an alien in a dangerous land.

CHAPTER 9—A CONCERT

Pain clutched my heart as I watched my grandfather struggling to make his way from his bedroom to the kitchen table after he'd agreed to have breakfast with me. He moved unsteadily, like a blind man in unfamiliar surroundings, balancing himself between walls of the hallway and on chairs and tables in the living room until he reached the kitchen table. It was an arresting scene. I tried to refrain from watching because I knew it was time for a walker, or wheelchair, and he would vehemently resist using either. I was just happy to see him moving about which was an indication to me that he wasn't giving up hope.

"Good morning, son." His voice fought to sound cheerful.

"How do you feel, Grandpa?" I asked, knowing full well what his reply would be.

"Fine! The smell of this food is so savory it could wake the dead." He said in his usual jovial manner.

He ate the western omelet in silence and only spoke when I sat down to eat.

"Finish the journal, yet?" He caught me by surprise and I had to juggle my thoughts before answering.

"No. Not quite ... ."

"What's taking you so long? I thought you'd be done with it by now."

I knew what the journal represented to him—a vicarious trip to the past, and his urgency to reach the end meant that he could have a final closure of this painful period and ultimately peace. I didn't want to dwell on the peace aspect because it had a dual meaning. If it meant peace as in death, it was unacceptable.

" I'm struggling to understand as I go along." I said, thinking it was a satisfactory reply.

"You haven't asked me to clarify anything lately," he said. "Where are you now?"

"I just finished reading the part where they burned your house."

He stopped eating, and his hand trembled as he raised the coffee cup to his lips. He stared at me as if waiting for me to repeat what I had said. Then his eyes clouded with mist, and he looked away.

"I think perhaps that was the saddest day of my life—watching that house burn. Years later, during the Civil Rights movement in America, I would just break down and cry when I saw pictures of Black homes and churches in the South being burned by hooded white men. Your grandmother would cry alongside me, but she had no idea how deeply personal it was for me. Later, we participated in the marches; yelling, screaming, and sometimes crying openly for due recognition and justice.

"It was my way of fighting back at injustice. Those hooded men in robes who openly terrorized Black people were not Nazis, but they were tainted fruit from the same tree, filled with the same hatred and violence. It felt good to have the freedom to do what I couldn't do in Germany."

"Grandpa," I said, not really wanting to ask the question on my mind, yet feeling that I needed to know. "Was it only after you had sex with Frau Benz that you knew you were in love with her?"

He looked at me and smiled. "No. You must remember I was at a young age in the beginning. It was after her husband and my father disappeared that I began to have mixed feelings. I didn't understand why I had the sudden warm, stimulating feeling in my sex organs when she hugged or kissed me. Now I know it was that time in a young man's life when his hormones begin screaming for some recognition. She was a mother figure to me, but many young boys have visions of having sex with their mothers. The first night we had sex was more of a coming-out as a man than the sexual gratification. It was a thorough lesson in the surging of manhood and my role as a man. I am deeply indebted to her today."

"Did you ever think of marrying her?

"Yes, but the Good Lord had other plans, which you will find out when you read further into the journal."

"Did you ever find out how your father was executed, and why did it matter <u>how</u> he was killed?"

"I just felt that my father didn't deserve to die a painful death. He was such a good, peace-loving man who, because of his background as a slave, was tenacious about the rights of people to live and enjoy life without impediment. But when I saw the lynching and murders during the Civil Rights movement, I visualized my father as being one of those Black Men hanging from a tree. They all died for a cause they believed in—freedom."

Grandpa had eaten everything I'd prepared; his eyes were droopy and his head had quick, jerky motions, as if he were trying not to fall forward.

"You wanna lie down and rest awhile, Grandpa?" I asked, rising to assist him.

"Yes, I think I ate too much." He extended his hands for the first time to accept my offer of help.

"I'll read more of the journal today, and when you wake up, we'll talk some more." I eased my arm around his waist and supported him to his bedroom.

Later, as I prepared to read more from the journal, I thought about the questions I had asked about his relationship with Frau Benz. They were purely personal to me. I was trying reach deep inside to understand my relationship with Sigrid. She was a sweet person, and I really didn't know how to characterize what I felt for her. Was it infatuation, love, or just friendship? "Maybe I just needed to be with her more for the feelings to materialize," I thought.

While Grandpa was asleep, I began reading where I'd left off in the journal.

<u>During the weeks that followed the murder of our loved ones and the savage destruction of our homes, Hilda and I found solace in each other's arms. Our neighbors in the farm community were very supportive. They donated furniture—bed frames, chairs, tables, and other household items they thought we needed or could</u>

use. Their benevolent gestures enabled us to cope with our tragic loss. But for me, the loss was catastrophic.

Notwithstanding the fact I had no living relatives in the world; I didn't exist. All documentation to support my legitimacy as a person and citizen of Germany had been destroyed by fire. I felt it was just another debilitating episode in my life, and I really didn't know how to cope with the deformity. I struggled to conceal my feelings. Even though I loved Hilda and Wolfgang, I decided it was a very private concern.

Obviously, Wolfgang had been watching me closely and knew what was on my mind, because one day we stopped work early, cleaned up, and donned fresh clothes. Then we went to the town of Harburg, which was the "Rathaus"(city hall), for several surroundings towns and villages—including Wilhelmsburg. We went directly to the office involved with birth records, passports, citizenships, and a host of other functions.

I sat in a pensive mode in back of the office, while Wolfgang marched up to the desk to talk to the lone occupant of the room. He was an elderly gentleman with stringy white hair, heavily furrowed face, and gold-rimmed glasses with thick lenses perched on the tip of his nose. His desk was covered with thick binders and endless piles of paper.

A dust covered light bulb hanging in the center of the high ceiling, was out, leaving the room shaded. A window, designed to provide sunlight and fresh air, was blocked by the new building next door.

Wolfgang spoke in sweeping gestures while the old man looked briefly in my direction, then back to Wolfgang's threatening hands and massive arms.

Then abruptly, Wolfgang looked to me.

"Hermann, come here."

As I approached the desk, the old man stared at my feet as if he were trying to guess my shoe size. Then his gaze moved slowly up my body and stopped just before meeting my burning gaze. He motioned for me to sit. With a writing pad in hand, he asked me questions.

"Name?"

"Hermann Hoffmann," I answered.

"When and where were you born?"

"Wilhelmsburg, June 9, 1925."

"Your father's name?"

"Also Hermann Hoffmann." I was beginning to feel uncomfortable because of the man's refusal to make eye contact with me. When he spoke, it was to my shirt, trousers, or shoes. When he stood and walked away from the desk, I whispered to Wolfgang, "I don't like this guy."

Wolfgang indicated he didn't either, but thought we should wait.

When he returned to his desk, he addressed his remarks directly to Wolfgang.

"We have no record of a Hermann Hoffmann being born in Wilhelmsburg in 1925. Regardless where he was born, the Third Reich's Citizenship laws of 1935 prohibits him from holding a German citizenship." He passed a sheet of paper to Wolfgang. "Article 2." He pointed to the paper. Wolfgang passed it quickly to me. I read the printed words under article 2:

(1) A citizen of the Reich is only that subject who is of German or kindred blood and who, through his conduct, shows that he is both desirous and fit to serve faithfully the German people and the Reich.

(2) The right to citizenship is acquired by the granting of citizenship papers.

(3) Only the citizen of the Reich enjoys full political rights in accordance with the provisions of the laws.

I looked at Wolfgang and nodded. The man was right. Suddenly, I noticed the thick layer of red veins popping up in Wolfgang's forehead. The man saw it too and began moving his chair quietly away from the desk and Wolfgang.

"Ah, just what is your interest in this... person?" he asked, cringing in his chair.

"He works with me on my farm." Wolfgang's voice roared like a vicious lion who is wary of an intruder approaching his lair.

"We raise the food that feed the soldiers of the Third Reich."

"Okay! okay." The man cried. "Why didn't you say so earlier? We can give him papers to remain here as an *Auslander* (foreigner) for one year, but he must stay and work on the farm with you. After one year, he must file for an additional year." He scrambled nervously through the cluttered desk and finally found what he was looking for. "Please fill this out, sir, sign it, and we will send the papers to your address."

Wolfgang looked at me. I nodded.

Months later, I received papers granting me permission to remain in the country of my birth, as a foreigner, for one year. But it didn't matter anymore. I had reached that point where I really didn't care who I was or where I came from. I was happy working on the farm. It was a profound sense of accomplishment when I planted seeds and watched the earth break open to release the food stems of life. And, even though the outside world had disowned me, I had the love and respect of two wonderful people. Wolfgang was like a brother, and Hilda was the tender love I'd never experienced.

During the weekends, spring, summer, and early fall, Hilda and I played music in front of our cabin, which had been refinished, redecorated, and made into a comfortable home. Children gathered from throughout the neighborhood to listen, frolic, and dance to our music.

One day a young girl, in her teens, arrived carrying a violin case. She sat quietly and listened until we had finished. Then with shy hesitation, she approached Hilda and asked if she could play with us.

Hilda was skeptical at first because of the girl's age, but then she realized, notwithstanding my size, I was still a teenager. Hilda asked her to play something, and we discovered that she was a musical genius. We were totally mesmerized by the enchanting sound flowing from her violin. We discovered she could also play cello and flute.

Her name was Gesla. She had a repertoire of works from most of the masters in classical music stored in her memory. She was reserved until she sat down and played music. Then the sad, bashful Gesla became a motion of sound, harmony, and smiles.

We didn't know much about her except she lived somewhere in the neighborhood. We were curious and asked Wolfgang. He explained that Gesla was the daughter of a mixed marriage. Her mother German; her father Jewish.

When her father disappeared during Kristallnacht, she was hidden by her mother and other farmers. Fearful that the Gestapo would come searching for her, she kept her luggage packed at all times and moved from house to house on a regular schedule.

With the new addition to our group, Hilda began writing special arrangements to include the flute. She extracted excerpts from the works of Brahms and Mendelssohn, and fused them together to fit our group. We still favored these composers over others because they were sons of Hamburg who, unfortunately, had to go to other countries to seek recognition for their work.

Our mini-concerts attracted children and adults from our village and other areas. Wolfgang became upset because too many strange people were crowding around his farmhouse. He decided to move us to a different location and give us a stage.

Between the roadway that edged through the front of the farming village and the Elbe River was a small tract of land littered with brush and debris. Wolfgang and other farmers cleared it, and on weekends, they parked an empty trailer in the center of the area. The empty trailer, with three wooden stools, became our stage. With dark, tranquil waters of the Elbe River as our backdrop, we sat uncomfortably on stools and played lively music. Farmers could sit in front of their homes and listen or gather around the trailer as others from outside the neighborhood did. It was probably the first outdoor concert ever held in Hamburg.

The concerts became a festive event on weekends as people danced and sang. Some of the more innovative farmers offered fruit and vegetables for sale. It became a virtual farmers market with music.

One day, as happy music flowed out to the crowd, a man came and stood before the trailer listening to our music. We knew he was a stranger—not from any of the local villages—because of the way he was dressed: suit, tie, and polished shoes. Gesla became visibly nervous because she thought he was a Gestapo looking for her.

During our break, the man approached Hilda. I grabbed Gesla by the hand and we moved swiftly through the crowd to Wolfgang's house. Once inside, we watched through the window. I held her tight, trying to calm the tremor of fear attacking her body.

When Hilda and the man had finished talking, they shook hands and he disappeared in the crowd. Hilda came immediately into the house and embraced Gesla to assure her that everything was okay.

"Who was he?" I asked.

"He's from the Hamburg's Cultural Ministry. He's trying to 'restore the cultural atmosphere in Hamburg.'" Hilda said with a sarcastic smile.

"You're kidding?" I said.

"No! He heard about us and wants us to help him."

Gesla spoke for the first time. "Did he mention why the 'cultural atmosphere' is badly in need of restoration?"

" No." Hilda shook her head at the cutting tone in Gesla's voice.

"Yeah, he's just too proud to admit that the 'cultural atmosphere' is dead because the very people who brought the cultural revolution to Hamburg, and maintained it for over a hundred years, have been chased away by the inhuman treatment of a racist society." Tears were forming in Gesla's eyes.

Hilda reached for Gesla's hand. "I know how you feel, dear. The three of us have suffered enormous pain and anguish from

Pogroms of the Third Reich. But I know that my husband, Hermann's father and your father, too, would be happy if we did something positive to help restore this tattered society. Let's think of it as a monument to our loved ones." We embraced and immediately felt better.

Hilda made the arrangements, and for the first time in many months, Gesla left the farm village and went into Hamburg. Even the farmers, who had been so involved in protecting her, agreed that fear should not be allowed to deprive her of sharing her gifted musical expression.

The audition was held in an old opera house that had been closed since *Kristallnacht*. I was delighted to see a piano, and when I sat down my fingers ran instinctively over the keys as if I had no control. We practiced several days together as piano, violin, cello, and flute ensemble, and we used music from our favorite composers Brahms, and Mendelssohn. But during the audition the director advised us to play more of Richard Strauss.

After weeks of rehearsing, we were ready to perform. There were others on the program: singers, musicians, and dancers. But there was no group as diverse as ours. In attesting to our versatility as musicians, we alternated on all the instruments, except flute, without any change in the quality of our music.

We received a standing ovation at the end of our performance, and as the audience cheered and cameras flashed, we ducked backstage. I was the only black person on the program. The tuxedo was too tight, and the stiff shirt collar was scratching and biting me as I ran into my dressing room and locked the door.

I could hear the cameramen outside in the hallway and down at Hilda's room. I knew she would handle everything and also protect Gesla.

I was overjoyed that I'd participated in my first professional concert. I felt my father was proud of me. But I had a fearful feeling of what might happen if my picture appeared in the newspapers with Hilda and Gesla. Past incidents, like the Olympic Games, Berlin police station, and the passport office, had provoked a feeling within me that I didn't belong amongst other human beings in our society. A compelling feeling of being ostracized in my own country was constantly with me.

The newspaper article the next day hailed the concert as a success and the first step toward the new cultural revolution in Hamburg. One sentence was denoted to our group, which had no name: "A very versatile and talented group with a promising future."

A month later, we were invited to participate in a special program that would be a tribute to Richard Strauss and his music. We agreed simply because we enjoyed playing music and performing before an audience.

The concert was billed as, "An Evening with Richard Strauss, by the Hamburg Ensemble."

That evening, as we waited to go on stage—we were the last act on the program—Hilda huddled the three of us together, and we held hands. We'd learned that Richard Strauss was in the audience.

"I know what you're feeling about playing for this man," she said. "He represents the Third Reich and everything that's bad and evil. I feel the same way you do. But let's just think about going out there, playing our music, and having fun. Nothing else matters. Okay!" We smiled and hugged each other.

When we were introduced and entered the stage, a thunderous applause greeted us. For thirty minutes, we attacked Strauss's music probably like it had never been played before. At the end of the show we had the usual standing ovation, but this time we were surprised when Richard Strauss, head of the music bureau for the Third Reich, walked onto the stage.

He shook the hand of the conductor and bowed briefly to the orchestra. Then he shook and kissed Hilda's hand.

While he stood talking to Hilda, my mind flashed to the stadium in Berlin and I viewed Jessie Owens facing Hitler. As I watched Strauss moving from Hilda to Gesla, a familiar surge crept upward from my stomach and lodged in my throat. He was talking to Gesla, whose face was the color of a freshly polished beet. I was next. While holding on to the edge of the piano for support, questions flared through my brain in painful waves and echoed like a sonic boom. Would he shake my hand? Would I be the second Black Man to be publicly embarrassed by Hitler and his mob? Could I physically restrain myself from lashing out? The feeling was so strong and compelling that I made an abrupt turn, walked away from my piano and off the stage. I had no idea what was happening behind me as I ran pass my dressing room and out the back door of the theater. Ripping the bow tie from my neck, I picked up speed. I was in the inner city of Hamburg, and I knew I had to get back to the farm. I just wanted to milk the cows—at least they respected me. I wasn't worried about Hilda; she would understand and also take care of Gesla.

As I ran, the cool night air filtered through my lungs and dissipated some of the explosive feelings inside. Then suddenly, the skies over Hamburg harbor lit up as if it were a New Year's Eve celebration. It was 1943, and Hamburg was being attacked from the air for the first time during the war. I stopped with concern about Hilda and Gesla's safety. It was then that I noticed a car with dimmed lights driving very slowly behind me.

Besides the wailing fire trucks and ambulances heading toward the docks, it was the only car on the street. I began walking at a leisurely pace, and each time I changed direction, the car followed. Terror seized me after I realized that I was wearing a tuxedo and had no identification on me. In my jumbled rush to get out of the theater, I'd left my clothes and identification papers in my dressing room. The bombs which had been exploding around the docks began raining down on the inner city. I could feel the street rumble under my feet like the aftershock of an earthquake. But my immediate problem was not with bombs but the car behind getting much closer to me. I thought of ducking into an alley in an effort to lose them, but the deafening sound of bombs exploding, sirens and screams, prevented me from making a quick decision. Before I could react, the car pulled along side me and stopped.

Two men in dark clothing and wide-brimed hats, stepped out. One stood in front of me and one behind. They asked for identification. When I told them I'd just finished playing a concert for Richard Strauss and foolishly left my wallet in my dressing room, they laughed and made jokes.

I heard the same vicious words I'd heard in Berlin, and all the self-restraint left in me was shattered. I reached instinctively for the man standing in front of me, but felt my head and neck explode from behind. The last thing I remembered was the vibrant sounds of night, as the hard, cold sidewalk, rushed upward to meet my face.

CHAPTER 10—A VISIT

It was midday, and Grandpa had slept late again. I was debating whether to wake him when I heard bumping and thudding sounds emanating from his bedroom. Creeping down the hallway, I crouched beside his bedroom door.

"Grandpa!" I waited. There was no answer. Hesitantly, I eased the door open. Grandpa was lying on the floor on his back with both hands folded across his chest. "Grandpa!" A bone of fear clogged my throat. Deep down inside I was silently praying, "move ... please move." His head turned slowly toward me, and he was smiling.

"Tripped myself when I was getting out of bed, son. I'm okay. Just help me up."

I rushed to him and the scene flashed poignant memories of me as a boy at summer camp. Near the camp was "Turtle Lake." We would go down to the lake in the afternoon and watch the old and young turtles crawl out of the water onto the sand. Each boy would pick his target, quietly creeping up behind the turtle and flipping it over on its back. We'd watch in laughter as the turtle struggled; grasping the air with its crabby little legs in a frantic plea for help. Finally, the turtle would retract its head and legs inside the safety of the shell until someone came along and flipped it back on its stomach.

That was the stoic picture of Grandpa, lying on the floor, waiting for me to come and pick him up. Using the Heimlich maneuver, I wrapped my arms around his body and felt the hardness of his ribs. He was losing his body fat and I knew it would only be a matter of time before he would have the hideous appearance of a skeleton with a thin layer of flesh. I sat him gently in a chair, and felt the recurring pains of sorrow. I knew instantly that I was going to get that wheelchair, whether he liked it or not.

Grandpa tried to make a joke of his little accident in the bedroom, and I realized it was time he got serious about his illness.

"Grandpa!" I heard the sternness in my voice. "We need to get serious about your illness. It's getting worse. I love you, Grandpa, and I'm concerned about you. We're going to make some quick changes, and the first thing is the wheelchair. Then I'm going to have a ramp built to the back door so you can go outside in the fresh air and sunshine. You may have given up on yourself, but I have not." He looked up at me with the compassionate plea of a wounded animal.

"Okay, son. Whatever you say."

That night we enjoyed a savory dinner—my special, broiled steak heaped with onions and crispy, deep fried potatoes. To top it off, we opened a bottle of California Sauvignon Red wine.

We laughed and told jokes, but it was apparent to me he'd finally, and reluctantly, surrendered himself to my care. We talked briefly about that part of the journal I had just finished.

"Grandpa, how did you feel when you discovered, according to the record, you had not been born?"

"Devastated. But you know, I was beginning to realize something—the incidents on the streetcar, the taunting by soldiers—I was different, and people don't like you if you're different. Since that day in Berlin, when the policeman called me a *Nigger bastard*, I thought about my reaction. It was something innate in me that was sparked by the humiliating tone of his voice. It sounded as if I wasn't supposed to be included in the human race. My father never talked to me about being different. When I returned from Berlin, I looked up the word *Nigger*, in a German dictionary and discovered it was the same word for *Mohr* (Negro). But when I crossed-checked it with an English dictionary, I discovered it to be derogatory and offensive. I was only a young boy, but an onerous question invaded my mind. Why should I be derogatory and offensive to anyone? It was a question that is still unanswered. So, the charge that I wasn't born when I *was* born was an evasive way to deny my existence.

I was invisible. The only time I felt like a real man—a human being—was on the farm with Hilda and Wolfgang. The love, respect, and admiration we had for each other transcended all boundaries of human existence. We were a living example of what the interaction of human species should be.

Even after my arrival in the United States, I felt invisible. White people looked through me as if I were not there. It was only after the Civil Rights movement that I forcefully made myself visible. I wanted everyone to look at me when talking to me."

"Can you explain Gesla's demeanor. Why was she so angry?"

"The Nuremburg Laws of 1935, which affected my status, also affected Gesla:

An individual of mixed Jewish blood is one who is descended from one or more grandparents who were racially full Jews.'

'Marriage between Jews and subjects of German or kindred blood are forbidden. Marriages conducted despite this law are invalid. Proceedings for annulment may be initiated only by the public prosecutor.'

After these laws were made public, Gesla's father suddenly became a victim and subsequently disappeared. And since she was Jewish, according to those laws, Gesla lived in fear they would find her and send her away. The distinction between her situation and mine was blatantly clear—she was told flat out 'we don't want you here.' In my case, they refused to acknowledge that black people resided in Germany and had been an integral part of the society since World War I. So you see, after Hitler came to power, we became invisible."

"Explain Gesla's remarks about the cultural restoration."

"Hamburg was never an intellectual center. The merchants of Hamburg were more concerned, during the early 1900, in using their considerable talents to make Hamburg into the third greatest port in the world, after New York and London.

"However, Jewish residents of Hamburg possessed a strong communal spirit that was as much identified with the needs of Hamburg as with their Jewish communities. Jewish foundations supported orphans, old people's home, hospitals, schools, and low-cost housing. They also, and this is what Gesla was alluding to, helped organize theaters, literary societies, and research institutes. And in 1938, all this began to collapse."

"Do you think Richard Strauss would have shook your hand?"

"As I reflect on it now, and I have had some soul wrenching thoughts about it through the years. Yes. He was a musician—a composer—and I think he was appreciative of the way we played his music. I think he was just like most of the German people who were reluctantly caught up in the hysteria of *Der Fuhrer* and his bullshit. But that night, as I watched him talking to Gesla, my mind became so overwhelmed with tainted reflections and images, that I just couldn't afford another embarrassment."

"Grandpa, I have some good news," I quickly made the transition from the journal. I received a call today from Sigrid. She and her family are in New York. They want me to come to the city and bring them out to meet you."

"Great!" He said, thrusting both hands in the air, as if claiming a much sort-after victory.

"Now I can finally find out just what is going on in my old country from the horse's mouth. Have you told them anything about me?"

"No."

"Good. We'll let it be a surprise and see what reaction we get."

I didn't know what Grandpa had in mind, but his face was all skewed up with happiness and anticipation, like a child preparing for bed on the night before Christmas.

When I spoke with Sigrid over the phone she said her father knew how to get from Manhattan to Kennedy Airport. So we agreed to meet somewhere near the entrance to JFK.

I saw them immediately after I'd made my exit from the expressway to enter into JFK. They were standing beside a bright red sports car and staring upwards at the stream of incoming jet planes, like huge kites evenly spaced on a long string extending through the clouds as far as the eye could see.

As I approached, the bright sunlight bouncing off the shiny surface of the convertible created multi-colored floating balls that temporarily blinded me.

Sigrid greeted me, when I stepped out of my car, with a brief hug and several firm pats on the back as if to welcome me into their elite club. She introduced me to her father who quickly extended his right hand. Between the fingers of his left hand was a long, handsome cigar —with at least three inches of dusty grey ashes clinging to the end like a circumcised penis. The ashes drifted to the ground during the firm handshake, and he stepped backward. His gaze rose to the sky.

He seemed annoyed that I had interrupted the serenity. Sigrid and her father looked like fashion models waiting to be photographed for a Calvin Klein's ad. He wore designer jeans and a denim vest covering a tan and black Pierre Cadin open-neck shirt. She wore glove-fitting jeans, burgundy thermal T-shirt covered by a burgundy brushed-cotton flannel shirt, hanging loosely down her willowy body.

"Where is your mother?" I turned to Sigrid and immediately noticed that this person was not the same Sigrid I knew at Juilliard. Her facial expression, boyish haircut, and mannerism appeared to be more masculine than the Sigrid I knew. "Maybe it was because she and her father was so *jeaned up*," I thought, "like the man in the cigarette commercial."

"Oh, she's running for a seat in the parliament and had to stay home and attend campaign rallies," Sigrid said.

As we drove away, her father followed me to Hempstead, and Sigrid rode with me. Several times, he became impatient with the speed I was traveling, swung his powerful Mercedes around my quiet, reliable Honda, and sped to the next parking area, then waited for us. He repeated this move three times before we reached the Hempstead exit.

When we arrived, Grandpa was sitting in the living room waiting. He was clean shaven, and decked in a fresh shirt and trousers. He was eagerly poised to greet the first guests we'd had in the house since Grandma's death.

He greeted Sigrid and her father in German. Then they began a spirited conversation in German, and I quickly slipped into the kitchen. I needed to make sure the cake and pastries were still fresh. I'd bought Sigrid her favorite—peach cobbler. At school, we'd found this quaint little coffee shop near Lincoln Center where she was introduced to peach cobbler. Many days and evenings we sat with a dish of rich cobbler and several inches of vanilla and chocolate ice cream piled on top. And the coffee—Sigrid always wanted to caress the coffee beans in her hand before they were ground.

"It makes my cup of coffee more personal," she'd said.

I had the coffee beans she liked, and a brand new coffee grinder. When I was satisfied everything was ready, I went back into the living room.

They were still speaking in German, but as soon as I sat down, the conversation shifted to English.

"Your grandfather speaks perfect German," Sigrid said.

"Yes, he was in Germany during the war." I didn't know what else to say. I had no clue to what Grandpa had told them in German.

Dr. Schiller, Sigrid's father, spoke.

"You didn't learn to speak German that well from being in the military." He pointed an unsteady finger at Grandpa. "Your German is *Hoch Duetsch* (high German). You speak it like you have roots in the language." He laughed, as if it were a preposterous joke.

"Yes," Grandpa said. I waited on the edge of my seat. This was the moment Grandpa was waiting for. "It was my first language. I was born 1925 in a small town outside of Hamburg." The room was in total silence, as if all voices in the world had been locked in a soundproof room. Sigrid and her father exchanged what appeared to be embarrassing glances.

"My father," Grandpa interrupted the silence, "was a slave in Germany during the late 1800s. He married a slave woman, and when they were free, settled in Hamburg. Later, my father became a professor at Hamburg University."

"Slavery in Germany?" Sigrid asked, while sliding back in her chair and shaking her head in disbelief.

"Yes, if you dig deeply into the history of that period, you'll find it's true," Grandpa said.

Dr. Schiller sat quietly.

"Daddy, you know anything about this?" Sigrid had a defiant look on her face.

"I remember reading something about it in my university studies," he said, and quickly changed the subject. "And you were in Germany during the war?" he asked Grandpa.

"I was there, but I didn't participate in it. I was one of those undesirables who surreptitiously ended up in a special concentration camp."

"*Special* concentration camp?" Dr. Schiller leaned forward in his chair, his gaze fixed on Grandpa.

"Yes, Hitler had a special camp for Black males near Mannheim."

There was heavy silence again in the room. Dr. Schiller was speechless, and Sigrid sat with her head down. Grandpa quickly changed the subject. "Are you a medical doctor?"

"Psychiatry."

"Good. You're the right person to answer my next question." Grandpa leaned forward, looking directly at Dr. Schiller. I could feel the impending tension in the room and it made me uncomfortable.

"Has Germany finally emerged from its inexorable period of guilt—about Hitler's legacy?"

"Yes. I think so." Dr. Schiller sat up quickly, eager to answer the question. "Perhaps there are still a few dissenting splinter groups, but I think after two decades of denial, the realization came that it was an indelible part of our history and we must accept it in order to move forward. I believe our recent economic prosperity can attest to that."

"Do you get any patients with post-Holocaust syndrome?"

"Not any more. Many years ago, when I first started my business, I had quite a few who were trying to mentally escape, and others—young men and women—trying to cope with the burdensome catastrophe committed by their country. It was particularly hard for members of my generation.

"When we were kids, no one talked about the past. At school, the teachers avoided any discussions about the war, or the horrors of the Holocaust. It was not only forbidden to ask but to even contemplate something so horrendous could have happened.

"It was only when I became a young man about to enter the university, that I began reading English writer's account of what happened during the war. I felt a deep sense of guilt and shame. I think that was the conclusive reason why I decided to study psychiatry. I wanted to find out why it happened. What kind of mentality was conferred upon my people that forced them to follow a blind and destructive ideology.

"There has been a significant change over the past twenty years," Sigrid rejoined the conversation. "Our education system has an influx of teachers from my father's generation and afterward. They realized what was missing in our history books and are now insuring that young students are introduced to Germany's sordid past under Hitler's regime. Some schools have mandatory studies, and take students on field trips to concentration camps. It was an enlightening experience for me when I was in school. But I never read about slavery in Germany."

"Dr. Schiller." Grandpa was ready again. "Here in America we call those born after the war Baby Boomers. In your case you would be *Nach Kreiger Kind* (after the war babies). How do you feel about all the money being paid out to survivors and families of non-survivors of the Holocaust?"

"This has long been a sore subject with me and many others like myself." Dr. Schiller spoke with some agitation in his voice, and his arms rose in a gesture supporting his dislike for the subject.

"We have paid billions of dollars in restitution and reparation to individual victims of Nazism and to Israel. A lot of that money came from coffers of the economy we built from the ruins of the Nazi area. My generation had absolutely nothing to do with the crimes of our parents and grandparents."

"So you don't think any claims should be paid to any group of people who suffered?" Grandpa asked.

"Well, I think some claims are legitimate. But there are some groups that are making claims of suffering that cannot be proven. But irresponsible lawyers and groups with misplaced ethical standards are encouraging people to file erroneous claims. It's impossible to check, and anyone who dares to try is immediately labeled as anti-Semitic."

"So if black survivors tried to file a claim they would automatically fall into those groups that lack sufficient proof?"

"Wait! Let me make myself clear. I'm not against claims being paid. What I am against is the sapping of money out of a prosperous economy that was built after the war. Now, what should have happened is the Allies: United States, Russia, England, and France, who plundered Germany at the end of the war, should have used everything left by Hitler to pay these claims. Hitler left enormous wealth scattered throughout Europe. What happened to it? Also, the German firms and institutions that were part of Hitler's regime, and still exist today, have the moral responsibility to make amends to anyone who suffered during the Holocaust. I believe some have already volunteered, but there are others who are trying to hide behind a legal facade to escape their responsibility. Granted, some of these organizations made significant contributions to the growth and success of Germany's economy after the war. Nevertheless, they should not be allowed to escape their moral responsibility for what happened during the war."

The exchange between Grandpa and Dr. Schiller was friendly, and I could see they were sharing some common beliefs.

For Grandpa, it was a closure on thoughts and feelings that had haunted him for many years.

"Dr. Schiller," Grandpa said, "you mentioned several times about you and your generation rebuilding Germany into one of the most prosperous economies in Europe. What about the *Gastarbeiters* (foreign laborers) who came to help rebuild Germany. What credit do they get?"

"Oh, I have the utmost respect and gratitude for the foreign workers who rebuilt only the infrastructure. We built the business that ignited the economy. Clearly, Germany has shown immense gratitude and respect to those workers—some are still living in Germany."

"But does that gratitude extend to citizenship?"

"No. And that's unfortunate because of an archaic law that links blood lineage to citizenship. While numerous changes have been made in the move toward democracy, some relics, like the citizenship laws, remain to haunt us. But that will soon change. As a matter of fact, my wife and her colleagues are working on such a change."

The conversation slowed, and Sigrid and I slipped out to get the coffee and cake.

I was delighted at the chance of finally being alone with her. But it felt different—not like the last time we were alone. I was awkward; kept dropping things and stumbling as if in a daze. She was overjoyed about the peach cobbler and coffee beans, but then she became somber. Her arms squeezed her body, and she breathe deeply.

"What's wrong, Sigrid?" I asked, watching her giving me a cold stare that told me doom was creeping into the kitchen.

"I have to tell you something, and I wanted to do it face to face. In school we never kept a secret from each other and now ... I've come so far to say it ... but... ."

"What is it Sigrid? You know you can talk to me." I said, feeling gloom and doom all around me.

"I'm gay." She said.

Whether it was doom descending or just the roof falling on my head, I survived long enough to say, "that's cool."

"Oh, Duke!" She hugged me warmly. She only called me Duke when she was incredibly happy. The name came from the times I imitated Duke Ellington on the piano. "I knew you would understand," she said.

"Have you found your <u>soul mate</u>?" I tried to make my voice sound supportive.

"Yes. Her name is Maria. We met when we played together with the Berlin Symphony Orchestra. She is a flautist. You'll love her."

"And your parents, do they know?"

"Yes, it's okay with my father, but my mother is in politics and ... well, you know. Maria and I are getting an apartment in Frankfurt, and you <u>must</u> come and visit."

The rest of the afternoon just floated by. Grandpa and Dr. Schiller had reached an impasse on the world's problems, and I felt as if I'd just lost my best friend. I told myself the torrid ache in my heart was only for the loss of my best friend.

When they drove away and Sigrid waved and smiled, I felt a part of my life had ended.

CHAPTER 11—THE TEACHER

Several days after Sigrid and her father had departed, Grandpa was still in a swaggering state of euphoria. He strutted around mumbling words and phrases in German. Seeing me watching, he'd stop and smile. The conversations in German had vicariously transported him to his old country. Sigrid and her father had provided the catalyst—the unbreakable link between him and the place of his birth. I wondered how I would feel being compelled to live in another country. Would I miss America? He'd lost both his parents, and to think of them was to undeniably think of Germany. It was an unforgettable episode in his life.

We hadn't discussed the journal for days. I was really trying to avoid reading the next part which I knew involved his incarceration. I knew it would be horrible, and I didn't think I was ready for it. My limited knowledge of what happened during the Holocaust was gained through films, photographs, and the written word. Those people involved were human beings and I had deep empathy, but it wasn't personal. Now that I'd discovered Black people were among those human beings, it suddenly became personal.

To keep Grandpa's spirits up, I visited a local travel agency and picked up a brochure on Hamburg, Germany. It was delightful to see the sparkle in his eyes and his hands shaking with excitement as he unfolded the brochure.

"It's so beautiful," he beamed, spreading the accordion-shaped brochure out on the kitchen table. "So many changes."

His fingers ran impatiently over the contour lines of the city map as if he were searching for something special. Abruptly, his fingers rested and he tapped the spot with quick nods of his head. "This is the town where I was born," he said, flashing the smile of a happy child. Then quickly folding the map, his smile faded. "What's happening with you and Sigrid?" His question caught me by surprise.

"Nothing." I said.

"Nothing? She's a very nice girl."

"Yeah, I know. But we're just friends. There is no involvement." I said, fighting the irresistible urge to tell him the whole truth, including how I really felt and probably would feel for the rest of my life. It was my first time being in love.

"Okay," he said, and slowly unfolded the map again as if I had suddenly become invisible. I acknowledged his desire for privacy and eased away.

Earlier, I had received notification from the high school reminding me about the first day of school. When I left Grandpa sitting at the kitchen table, my mind was courting fantasies of being a teacher. It was my first step toward becoming a professor.

Professor, was a title that preceded the names of my great grandfather, grandfather, who taught at Juilliard, and my father, who taught political science at Columbia University. Now, it was my turn. My plan included teaching a year or two at the high school, then entering a Master's of Music program at Juilliard. That would be the gateway through which I could achieve and uphold the prestigious title of <u>Professor</u> in the family.

When I left the following morning for school, Grandpa was still sleeping. We'd toasted with champagne the night before to my first day as a teacher, and I believe he drank a little too much.

Driving onto the school grounds, I followed the bold arrow signs pointing to the faculty parking area. The morning sunlight was gentle, the air pristine. It was that time of year when the sun confirmed the passing of summer, and the morning and evenings were cool and comfortable, signs that fall was about to invade Long Island.

Students gathered around the school in groups—yelling, singing, and horsing around. I thought of my high school days and how happy I was to return to school after summer vacation. It was exhilarating just being away for a few months, but nothing could compare to coming back to romp and clown with friends and comrades, and especially to harass the teachers.

I was politely informed by a person at the information desk that the first thing on the program was an assembly that I had to attend. About the same time, a loud clanking of the school bell reminded everyone that school was in session, and students began overflowing the building with mumbling sounds of protest that were universal on the first day of school.

I was escorted by the same person at the information desk, and managed to avoid the mass of students moving aimlessly through the corridors. We entered the backstage of the auditorium where a group of adults sat in a semicircle on stage.

I spotted Mr. Saberstein who waved. I knew then that the non-smiling adults had to be faculty members.

The ethnic makeup of the faculty had the appearance of a delegation to the United Nations. Mr. Saberstein hastily shook my hand, and with his florid salesman's smile, pointed me toward my seat. Looking out at the students filing into seats, I felt a surging wave of emotion. They were indeed a diverse group of students, and I found myself involved in a mental configuration of the different cultures represented. My mental thoughts were quickly translated into a harmonious combination of tones that could emerge from those students playing their native music. I felt a shiver of excitement at the prospect of teaching a group of music students with such varied cultural and ethnic backgrounds.

Mr. Saberstein was at the podium trying unsuccessfully to quiet the students. He spoke about school programs, but spent most of his time on rules, regulations, and the consequence of noncompliance. Then he introduced the teachers. It was interesting to hear, as the teachers were introduced, the applause given to the favorite teachers and the deadening silence given others. My name elicited a thunderous silence. But I realized that most of those teachers who received such silence were possibly the best teachers who demanded discipline and respect in the classroom. As for me, I just had to prove myself.

I was escorted by a person from logistics to my classroom, a lone building—away from the main building—out near the sports field,.

The inside had the open space of a gymnasium, but instead of athletic equipment music instruments lined the walls and covered most of the floor space.

"You are responsible for all of this," the man with the clipboard tucked gingerly under his arm said in a sweeping gesture with his hand. "No one should take an instrument outside this building unless it is signed for by the individual taking it out."

Mentally, I was trying to calculate the dollar value of the instruments. There were enough instruments to equip two or more bands.

"You have half-a-million dollars worth of instruments in here," the man said, "some are brand new. We can't seem to get enough students interested in playing music. It's a damn shame ... all our tax-paying dollars just going to waste. I just don't understand the mindset of our kids today. How can anyone not like music? When I was in high school all I had was a leaky B-flat trombone." He was looking at me hoping to elicit some endorsement for his complaints.

I had no remarks, although I knew he was right. I just stood in awe of all those music instruments—some still encased with tight metal bands. It was frightening to think of the enormous responsibility I was undertaking. In the back of my mind seeds of doubt were trying to sprout warning stems.

My first week as a teacher was frustrating and profoundly depressing. I had only four new students. The regular students came primarily from junior and senior classes. They were the only participants in the school band, which some aptly described as more of a school combo.

With two and three years behind them, they were frustrated and disillusioned about playing music. For most, it was only the credit they cared about.

"We come to music period because it's a chance to get away from other grueling subjects," said one student.

"When we come here, we get a chance to play—maybe a half-hour of music—then we're relaxed and ready for the rest of the day," said another.

"We don't like the frickin' music policy here." A student stood up, his glaze glancing around for approval from the rest of the group. When he was assured he had approval, he continued to speak. "We think it stinks. There is no enjoyment in playing music. When Mr. Nichols was here, it was a lot of fun to play." The crowd was becoming vociferous in support of their sagging music program and the student continued his outcry.

"Mr. Nichols gave us permission to experiment with different types of music so we could get a feel for the rhythm and harmony. We learned a lot, but then he got fired. We used to have a big school band and competed with other schools. That's all gone. Do you know jazz, Mr. Hoff?"

His fellow classmates applauded when he sat down. They seemed relieved that he had boldly articulated their pent-up feelings. Now, they were looking to me for a solution. I didn't give an answer about the jazz question, I simply nodded.

After class was over, I sat at my desk and stared at the spacious building and all the instruments—with names and serial numbers plainly attached—like unknown dead bodies waiting at the morgue for someone to claim them, and I felt like screaming, "What a waste... what a fucking waste."

That night, I discussed the situation with my grandfather. He listened intently, and when I had finished spewing my anger, he spoke calmly to me.

"Son, you're beginning to learn some crucial things about life." He was looking directly at me, and instantly I knew he was serious. "Most people think the path of righteousness is one straight line from A to Z. And if you walk that line you'll probably reach Z, then die and go to heaven. But it's not that easy, and only when a person has traveled that path can that person speak with any credibility about it." He was still looking at me as if he wanted me to acknowledge that he had indeed traveled that path. I nodded for him to continue.

"There are lots of pitfalls and numerous forks on that path. These are the challenges we face in life. We are also faced with choices ... should I detour from the path, or should I continue straight ahead? Only you can make the decision for your life. If you choose to detour and meet some of these challenges, then it's your choice. It doesn't necessarily mean you will never reach Z, it means it will just take a little longer to arrive. But if you believe in yourself and the choices you make, you'll arrive safely. You understand what I'm trying to tell you, son?"

"Yes, Grandpa, I believe I do." Grandpa's face had acquired a mystical shape, and I found myself digesting his words of wisdom.

The next day, I was waiting outside Mr. Saberstein's office when he arrived.

"Good morning, Mr. Hoff. How was your first day of school?" His gaze told me he didn't want to be bothered.

"Horrible, Mr. Saberstein." I wanted my voice to sound polite, yet resolute. "That's why I'm here to talk with you."

He opened the door to his office and turned to face me. "Okay, come on in." The sound of his voice, and the look on his face were clear evidence he'd rather be doing something else.

In wordless silence, I sat and watched as he preceded to do what must have been his daily ritual: meticulously hanging his jacket on the coat tree, checking his appearance in the mirror on the inside of the door to his private restroom, sifting through messages on his desk, and finally sitting down in the plush leather chair behind his desk.

"Well, Mr. Hoff. What's the problem?"

I'd waited so long that I almost forgot my prepared opening statement.

"Mr. Saberstein..." I stammered. "I had four new students yesterday."

"So?" He pumped his palms upward, urging me to continue.

After the first few words I was ready. "Mr. Saberstein, do you know how much money has been spent on musical instruments for your school?" I didn't give him a chance to answer. "Half a million bucks ... dollars ... moolah. And did you know that most of the instruments are still in their original packing—new—never used?" I felt I was on a downhill roll with the wind at my back. "And do you know why you don't have a school band like most other high schools, and have not had one for the past two years? And lastly, do you know that after this year you probably won't have enough students to support your music program?" I stopped, waiting for him to crawl from under the pile of debris I had just thrown over him.

"Just what is your point, Mr. Hoff?" He was trying to don his suit of armor, but his eyes betrayed his concern. I knew that what I had just said was beginning to wrinkle Mr. Saberstein. Now that he'd been heaped with debris, I was ready to light the fire.

"My point is simple. The reason you don't have a music program is you!" The burning tip of my finger was pointed toward his face. "Have you ever *talked* to your students besides telling them what they can or cannot do? I talked to the few music students who showed up for class. They are unhappy, frustrated, and disillusioned with learning. You have set the rules and regulations to meet your specific goals—not theirs. They are not having any fun—freedom to explore the wonders of learning—"

"Mr. Hoff!" He stood up. I could see the veins growing rosy on his forehead, and spreading to the balding area just before his receding hairline.

"Everything I do here at this school, is in the best interest of the majority of my students. All programs, and activities are designed for the student's advancement. Those who grumble are certainly in the minority."

"Mr. Saberstein, I've been reading a lot about Hitler and his influence on the majority of the German people during his tenure. He had undoubtedly convinced them that everything <u>he</u>

was doing was in the best interest of the German people. It was a very persuasive commitment. But you and I, and the whole world know it was deception."

"I don't appreciate you comparing me to Hitler, Mr. Hoff. However, I acknowledge the intended analogy." He walked away from his desk and out of my sight line. "Just what do you propose I do to reverse the situation in the music program?" He sounded deflated, and I felt he was reaching out for help. I turned to answer and he was standing in front of his array of certificates spaced on the wall.

"Give me full control over the music program." I said with vigor. "Let me recruit students and establish a program where students can enjoy themselves as they learn and grow."

"Okay!" He turned to face me, then moved toward the door. "You have until spring break to improve the music program. If not ...you're fired. Good day, Mr. Hoff." He opened the door and pointed his finger toward the hallway.

CHAPTER 12—THE CAMP

Grandpa was thrilled with his new wheelchair. The dual functions provided him the option of manually moving himself around, or using the battery-powered motor. When in my presence he preferred to maneuver himself around, but I had a strong feeling he experimented with the motor when he was alone.

He congratulated me on my decision with Mr. Saberstein.

"You made your stand. I think it was a courageous act. Now, you must produce to maintain your credibility. Are you having any reservations about facing this challenge?"

"No, Grandpa. I really believe I can make a difference. Music is my love—my profession. I'm happy playing music, and I think I'll be happy teaching. Those kids are the future of music, and I believe they deserve the best we can offer."

"I'm proud of you son." He gestured for me to give him a hug. "When are you going to finish the journal?" I had anticipated he would soon get back to the journal and I was prepared.

"Tonight, Grandpa. I'm going to read some more."

I stepped back from the withering body of my grandfather and had to fight back tears. He was deteriorating rapidly, and I knew I was battling with time. It was so frustrating to just stand by and watch this horrible disease systematically squeeze the life out of my grandfather. It wasn't fair, I thought. But then I remembered something my mother taught me, "God is a fair and just God. Whatever he does is warranted and justified." Looking at Grandpa, I thought about the suffering of others, and was convinced that God was definitely in charge.

As I'd promised, after dinner I sat in my bedroom and opened the journal, removed the bookmark, and heard my grandfather's voice through the words:

I didn't know whether it was the thunderous sounds in the distant, the yelling and screaming, or the painful ache in the back of my head that awoke me. But when I opened my eyes and saw a luminous flashing of light, immediately followed by a thunderous roar, it reminded me of the times on the farm when the sky would suddenly transform into a huge black blanket, blotting out all light. Then lightening would streak perilously across the blanket, like an artist splashing bright luminous paint across a black canvas. The deep rocky roar that followed was a decisive warning to get off the field and find safe cover because the black canvas was about to unblock the dam and open the flood gates.

I expected water to shower down and drench my body with coolness, but it didn't happen. I lay on my back staring upward into darkness. I felt paralyzed; my body floating helplessly in a sea of darkness. Slowly, my sensibilities returned and I tried wriggling my toes, then my fingers. The connection was still in tact. I raised my right arm up and across my face, but I couldn't see it. My first inclination was, I had to be blind. I was flat on my back in a world of blackness.

Despite the unbearable pain behind my head, my mind eased into gear and flashbacks occurred. I remembered the concert— Hilda and Gesla, the bombing, the physical confrontation with the two men in dark clothing, and then total blackness. I raised both feet and kicked wildly in the air, but I couldn't see my feet. Terror snared my brain and I spoke without realizing it, "I'm blind. Oh, God, I'm blind." I noticed that my voice was all I could hear. What happened to the thunder and lightening? What happened to the screaming and yelling I'd heard earlier? I waited. No sounds. Then, as if on command, the blasting sound of a siren shattered the darkness with several short echoing bursts. And immediately, white, blinding flashes of light came on around me. Instinctively, I covered my eyes because I felt it was a giant explosion and I was seated in the middle of it. Suddenly, the sound of footsteps and voices danced in my eardrums. I removed my hands and realized, to my delight, that I had been in the middle of a total blackout. I wanted to shout with happiness after the realization that I wasn't blind. I was alive after a massive bombing raid on Hamburg.

But as my gaze moved about the small room, cold terror gripped me. I was in a cell. I jumped up from the damp, cement floor; my tuxedo was wrinkled and torn, my white shirt looked as if it had been passed through a shredding machine. The ache behind my head increased in severity as I stood up. But apparently from my upright position the blood flow increased, and the ache began to subside. Staggering, I reached the bars and slid to the floor.

The memory of seeing my father leaning against the bars the way I was angered me. "Hello! hello!" I yelled through the bars. No answer, just the sound of voices yelling in the distant. The cells opposite mine and across the hallway were empty. It seemed as if I were the only prisoner.

I sat down with my back against the cold and silent brick wall in back of the cell. I told myself I would wait. Someone had to come, eventually.

While waiting, my mind replayed the tapes of my past. It was a sinking realization that my life was slowly coming to an abrupt end. I had lost all my support along the way—my father, Hilda, Wolfgang. I was alone. One young Black Man alone against the evils of the Nazis. What would they do to me, I wondered. I had no identification. Maybe they would charge me with being a spy for America or England. Maybe I would meet the same fate as my father; nothing would surprise me. What I had witnessed over the past several years was incomprehensible. I wondered if it was just my bad luck to be born at the wrong time and place. I just hoped that Hilda and Gesla had escaped the bombing and were alive. If they didn't hear from me, they would assume I was dead and continue playing their music.

I have no idea how long I sat replaying the tapes and feeling the whole world had become bitter and cruel. I was an outcast, ostracized by society and hunted down by evil men with only one goal—to destroy me.

I could hear groans in the pit of my stomach; my throat was dry, and I had a pulsating urge to piss. I felt that if I moved at all it would trigger a flood of hot urine down my pants.

There were no toilet facilities in the cell, and I kept thinking that I should spray the walls. But I guess the care and respect I learned from my father about other people's property, restrained me. Then, like a cool breeze on a hot, muggy day, I heard footsteps. I rushed to the bars and watched helplessly as a man passed without looking in my direction or listening to my pleading that I needed to go to the bathroom. I heard the door slam behind him and I turned sharply and uttered, "please forgive me, Dad." I pulled out the hose and sprayed the walls of my cell.

With hunger and thirst taking turns debilitating my body, I sat propped up with my head resting against my knees. Waves and waves of dizziness swept over me. My mind kept tossing me the idea that I must live, but there was no motivation nor inclination to do so. All the energy and self-assurance that had been stored since I started working at the farm, were being wrenched like water from a damp mop.

The Nazis had found a convenient way to destroy me without using physical brutality. They would simply starve me to death. Somewhere in this negative thought process, I passed out.

When I felt the cool, soothing water raining over my head and down around my face, I realized I was still in a world of the living. My hands cupped automatically to catch some water to drink. Through partially closed eyelids, I saw the shoes—two pairs—black and highly polished. Black, baggy trouser legs flopped over the shoes. I thought of the two men who came to Wolfgang's farm and told him he had to produce more farm products to support the war efforts, and the men Gesla lived in fear of, and the two characters that picked me from the street. "Gestapo bastards," Wolfgang had called them.

My eyes opened fully and my gaze moved up the trouser legs to the slouching grey jackets, white shirt, black tie, and finally the wide-brim hats that shaded steel-cold eyes. They didn't speak. One dropped a loaf of black bread at my feet. The other one pitched a round ball of "*fleisch*" (meat), that bounced off my head. They walked away leaving a half pail of water in the middle of the cell floor.

I ate everything and then explored the floor for crumbs I may have dropped. If this was going to be my last supper, I had made the most of it, I thought. To be sure, I searched my clothing for hidden pieces of food. The hunger pains disappeared, but the abrupt appearance of the Gestapo was troubling.

I knew about Heinrich Himmler's secret police and their ruthless methods of searching out so-called enemies of the state. I didn't have too much time to ponder the problem before they reappeared and tossed a bundle of clothing through the bars. "*Anziehen*" (put these on), they yelled.

The bundle contained a pair of black trousers, a black wool shirt, and a black ski mask. I slipped into everything except the ski mask. I wondered why everything was black. I really didn't need all that black stuff to be concealed, I thought. Just turn off the light, and presto! I'm invisible. The thought was funny, but the sound of approaching footsteps made the joke ever so somber.

Two men came into the cell. I was holding the ski mask in my hand. One of the men grabbed it and fitted it snugly over my head.

"Let's go!" he said.

I thought about the notorious reputation of the Gestapo—a secret police organization that assumed control over the lives, freedom, and property of all Germans. It used any method it deemed necessary for the annihilation of enemies of the Third Reich. The warning my father gave me about speaking out because they would hunt me down, had no foundation. I had said nothing. My music had been my voice. Why me?

The two men, each grasping a strong hand under my armpits, practically lifted me off the floor and carried me from the cell. I weighed nearly two hundred pounds, but felt like a pendulum swinging between their strong bodies.

When the ski mask was jammed over my head the cut-outs, intended for the eyes, nose, and mouth, didn't exactly line up. So I couldn't see where I was going until I was shoved into the back seat of a car and the doors locked. As the car moved forward, I used my hands to ease the ski mask down into focus. We were leaving the city. Soldiers and policemen were everywhere; directing the mass exodus of people and cars leaving Hamburg. Some streetlights were out, and the blinding headlights of cars and trucks created deadlock traffic jams everywhere. The car I was riding in must have had some recognizable external symbols because it was given the right-of-way by soldiers and policemen at intersections where there were no functioning traffic lights.

I was surprised that I wasn't tied up or chained. Of course there was no place I could go, and the man opposite the driver turned to look back each time I moved. Looking at the size of the two men convinced me that it was a fit of rage that prompted me to attack them the night I was stopped. It was either rage or stupidity.

I thought of the covert rumors told about people disappearing while in custody of the Gestapo, and the fear prowling in my body shivered. I wanted to pull the ski mask off because tiny balls of sweat were sliding down my neck, and the vapor created from the incessant smoking by the two men made it difficult to breath. I tugged quietly at the bottom of the mask material trying to vent some space and allow air pockets to keep smoke from lodging in the material. I finally managed to get some ventilation, then realized I needed a gas mask for the smoke.

Soon, we were out of the city and traveling at very high speed. I tried vainly to see where we were—to spot some landmark that I could identify with—but everything was dark and unfamiliar. I knew we had to be on the Autobahn because of the speed, and we were not meeting any on-coming traffic. Suddenly, a chilling thought grazed through my mind causing saliva to back up in my throat, "They were going to hang me." That's why they gave me the ski mask. I remembered seeing movies where the condemned prisoner was led to the place of hanging. A black head covering was placed over his head, followed by a rope with a huge decorative knot. The rope was adjusted around his neck, and on a command he was dropped through the floor and bounced off the air below several times before he was still. The image froze me. It was no longer warm in the car.

My thoughts scattered, but fear intensified when the car slowed and we turned off into a wooded area. The car moved slowly. I could see a haze of light in the gloominess ahead of us.

When we stopped I recognized a railroad station, but the name of the town was unfamiliar. They pulled me out of the car, removed the ski mask, blindfolded me, and replaced the ski mask. The mystery, and apprehension was sapping all my courage. Where was I going? Why the blindfold?

I was taken inside the station and immediately felt there were others like me inside; the diverse body odors, the hushed sounds—unlike the echoes of an empty room, sent comforting waves through my body.

It was a feeling like you get when you're at a party and there is no one in the group of obnoxious people you know. Then you spot someone who is groping through the crowd like you, and you feel comfortable knowing you're really not alone.

"*Sitzen*" (sit), I was told, and for the first time my hands were secured behind me to the wall, or some other immovable object. I could hear low talk and whispers from bodies that I sensed were close around me. I tried to identify the different dialect, but I had little experience since I'd spoken German the same way since birth. But I was aware that people in other parts of Germany spoke with a different tone and inflection in their speech. I had no problem identifying the Bavarian dialect because I enjoyed the music and songs that came out of Munich. From the voices, I had a feeling there were people from different parts of Germany in the same room. Were they all black? There was no way to tell.

"*Ruhe! kein sprechen*" (quiet, no talking), was the bellowing command and the room was so still I could hear the sheltered beat of my heart.

After what seemed like hours of sitting with the blindfold compacting my eyeballs, I heard the sound of a train approaching and the low hissing of the engine as it slowed and stopped.

"*Aufstehen*"(standup), was the command, followed by the harsh reverberation of groans, rattling of chains, and movement of weighted feet. My hands had been detached from the object behind me, and I was led forward like a blind man following the leash of his seeing-eye dog. I stumbled several times and my aching toes told me I was crossing railroad tracks. And then I was seated in a coach.

The antiseptic smell from the seat covers reminded me of the last time I was on a train when I went to Berlin to visit my father in a jail cell. The premonition I had before going into that police station was certainly true. I wondered if I would get another magical flash for the situation at hand.

The slow, shuffling of feet, and the repetitive command to "sit" told me the coach was filling up with people. I was in a seat alone, but my hands were still tied behind my back and anchored to the back of the double seat. Remembering the seating arrangement on the last train ride, I decided I was seated by a window and tried leaning my head against the cold glass to calm my shattered nerves. I kept wondering what I would do if I had to go to the bathroom.

As the train inched forward, I sat back in my seat and thought about my destination. It had to be a concentration camp. But why all the secrecy? Why didn't they just line us up and herd us out like I saw them doing in Berlin? On the farm, Hilda, Wolfgang and I, had many discussions about the undisputed rumors of the horrors going on in camps like Sachenhausen, Buchenwald, and Dachau. Many Germans dismissed the rumors as mere propaganda. I had my doubts because I couldn't believe it could happen in our society.

One rumor, which wasn't very interesting at the time, but one I was suddenly giving some thought—was the colored triangles each inmate had to wear: political prisoners wore red; criminals, green; shiftless persons, black; homosexuals, pink; Gypsies, brown; Jews, yellow. Blacks, as a group, were left out, so I just imagined they would add some ridiculous color like purple, for me.

While on the farm, I felt safe. We could discuss candidly the war, Hitler, the Gestapo, and anything else without fear of retaliation.

Now, I was anchored to a seat on a train taking me to an unknown destination and possibly death. I could feel the train slowing down, and tension gripped my body. When the train came to a full stop, the droning of truck engines and loud voices could be heard. Military commands were barked. Soldiers! I thought. We were being turned over to the military. A deep throated voice gave the command to board the train, and the onrushing of footsteps entered the coach. A second command was given to unlock the chains, and instantly, my hands were free—numb—but free. Then came the humiliating blow. I had no doubt who was riding the train with me after I heard that same command voice say: *"Aussteigen, Schwarze Hund"* (get off you black dogs).

* * *

I stopped reading the journal because of the intense anguish building inside my body, making comprehension extremely difficult. Those scenes of Grandpa's forceful abduction were particularly disturbing. I also needed to get some sleep because a very aggressive day awaited me at school.

Before leaving the following morning, I prepared breakfast for Grandpa. Normally, he ate only toast and coffee, but sometimes he wanted ham or boiled eggs. I always tried to place everything within easy reach from the wheelchair so he wouldn't have to stand up or reach across the table to get what he wanted.

Four slices of wheat bread stood ready in the toaster. Two hard-boiled eggs and thin slices of ham wrapped in foil, lay in a dish, and a pot of coffee sat on the percolator with the heat turned to low keeping it warm enough to drink but not hot enough to burn.

In the afternoon, when I returned from school, Grandpa was outside sitting in his wheelchair at the bottom of the ramp leading to the back door. As I slid out of the car, I sensed something was wrong. He was sitting with his head down, and although it was early fall and the sun was shinning brightly, it was cool enough for a jacket or sweater. Grandpa was wearing only a short-sleeved shirt.

"Hi, Grandpa."

He looked up and smiled. It was a thin smile which reinforced my feeling that something was wrong.

"I was just enjoying the sunshine," he said, extending both hands toward me. I grasped his hands and bent to kiss his forehead. He was shivering. His hands and forehead were cold, like a thin sheet of ice. Pulling off my jacket, I wrapped it around his shoulders.

"I better get you inside. Why did you stay outside so long?"

"It's such a nice day."

That wasn't exactly true, because when I reached the door it wouldn't open. He'd locked himself out of the house. I immediately thought of *memory loss*—two words Dr. Simon had emphasized that were directly related to Alzheimer's disease. But in my quick denial, I rationalized by thinking of numerous times I'd walked out of the house without my car keys.

Once inside the house I made some herbal tea, and spiked it with a shot of Bacardi rum. He drank it down and wanted another cup.

"Grandpa, I read some more of the journal last night."

"You did!" He perked up.

"Yeah, and I wanna tell you, I was really scared."

He looked at me with a blank stare as if he were trying to figure out what I was talking about.

103

"The Gestapo, Grandpa. When you were picked up by the Gestapo."

His gaze moved away from me and focused on the wall. Then he said sharply, "Oh, yeah. That was really scary."

I sat down opposite him and looked deep into his eyes. They were wide and fixed. I decided to ask him some questions to see if mentally he was still with me.

"Grandpa. Who bombed Hamburg, and was there much damage to the city?"

"The British," he said without hesitation and looked directly at me. His eyes were sparkling, like a lost person who'd just found something recognizable. I knew then he was still with me. "Yeah, they hit and destroyed the harbor. I learned later that the inner city was devastated. Lots of people died. I don't know about the town where I was born, or Wolfgang's farm, because they were on the outskirts of Hamburg. My, God, that was quite a night. I never wanna go through another time like that."

"Tell me more about the Gestapo. I've seen war movies and I'm confused about the difference between the SS and the Gestapo."

He sipped slowly from his cup—savoring the spiked tea— and like a historian about to recount events of past history, leaned back in his wheelchair and opened up his mind.

"The SS (Schutzstaffel—defense echelon), was a paramilitary group when Hitler came to power. They became his bodyguards. But later, Heinrich Himmler, persuaded Hitler to consolidate the functions of the SS and Gestapo. The primary functions of the SS were to administer all concentration camps. The Gestapo was a secret police force dedicated to the task of maintaining Hitler's regime. Hitler wanted a political police force that would protect the existence of the Third Reich, and also track down and eliminate all dissidents, complainers, and opponents. Hitler regarded an individual, no matter what his status, as a potential suspect."

Grandpa took a long sip of his tea, and I had a fleeting thought that perhaps the rum was good for his memory. Or, perhaps it was the total herbal connection that was revitalizing his memory.

"The Gestapo organization," he continued, "became the most important security organ of the state. I guess you can compare it to our FBI. It was completely autonomous, with its own legal system. It could, and did, use any method it deemed necessary to protect the state. It hunted down Jews and other political dissidents, interrogated and imprisoned anyone who told an anti-Nazi joke. Their methods were crude, but effective.

Any person suspected of opposition to Hitler's regime was first given a warning, and if that didn't work, he was taken into custody—for security reasons. The usual punishment was assignment to a concentration camp. If the person was considered really dangerous, he was arrested, interrogated, and often beaten to death."

Grandpa paused again and raised his cup. I decided to give him two shots of rum.

"The Gestapo," he began again, "extended its activities throughout Europe and even to distant parts of the world. For example, it followed the German Armed Forces into occupied countries and used its proven methods to destroy all elements hostile to Nazi rule. The Gestapo was responsible for the extermination camps in Poland. Everywhere, the Gestapo was regarded as one of the crudest police force of modern time."

Grandpa's speech was becoming repeatedly slow and slothful, as if he were suffering from a sudden energy loss. I knew I had to hurry, or I would lose him to the rum.

"After you were arrested, did you, at any time, think of trying to get away?" I asked, my words making a hurried exit before the door closed, severing our communication.

"Hell, no. Everything I just told you about the Gestapo, I learned from Wolfgang. He told me, 'Hermann, If you ever get picked up by those bastards, never, never try to get away. They will gladly kill you.'"

" On the train, did you have an intrinsic feeling that the rest of the people with you were also black?"

"I think so. I'd never been in a group of all Black folks before, except in school, and there were only a few Black kids. But sometimes we would all sit together. It was a special feeling—an intimate bonding that I didn't get with my other friends."

"I've read about concentration camps like Dachau and Auschwitz. Where were Sachenhausen and Buchenwald located?" It was my last question and I wondered if he could answer it. His head bobbed several times as if he were sleeping, but then jerked upward when I spoke.

"What did you say, son?" I repeated the question.

"Oh! Sachenhausen was a camp north of Berlin. It was originally set up as part of a penal system. Buchenwald was located in central Germany. It too, started out as part of a penal system, but soon became an extermination factory by means of starvation, beatings, tortures, over-crowding conditions, and sickness. The inmates were also required to work in factories, providing armaments for the German army. Buchenwald was the largest camp in Germany."

Grandpa's head drooped and his chin rested gently on his chest. His fingers lay limp over the arms of his wheelchair. I covered him with a blanket and took away his tea cup. The tea and rum were only a temporary remedy, I thought, but I had plans of using it again.

Later, after I'd finished preparing dinner, he was still sleeping. I wheeled him to his bedroom, moved him onto his bed, and returned to eat my dinner.

After dinner I sat watching television, and during the scenes where speech was replaced by music or silence, I distinctly heard voices emanating from a different source. I lowered the volume, but still heard voices. Turning the TV off, I followed the sound to Grandpa's room. Pressing my ear against his bedroom door, I could hear him having a spirited conversation with someone. After hearing the name, Lucy, I rapped lightly on the door.

"Come in!" it was Grandpa's voice.

Remembering the bathroom scene, I was hesitant about opening the door, but I did.

"Hello, son. Your Grandma is here." His voice had an unequivocal sound of truth, and his smile radiated confidence.

I stood frozen in the doorway. His gaze was fixed directly on the foot of the bed. I followed an imaginary line from his eyes to the foot of the bed, but there was no one at the foot of the bed. I looked around the room. Desperation swooped down like a vulture. I wanted to find something—anything that I could identify with Grandma.

"She's here, son," he pointed to the foot of the bed. I looked again. There was no one. Not knowing what else to do, I surrendered to the panic smothering me. I couldn't just say, "There is nobody at the foot of the bed, Grandpa." I opened my mouth but only empty air gushed out.

"Lucy, honey, your grandson is doing some wonderful things at his school. I'm so proud of him. Son, say hello to your Grandma."

"Hello, Grandma," I said, the awkwardness in my voice screamed for her reply. There was no reply. I looked at Grandpa, and he spoke.

"She's so happy about what you're doing at school with the music program, and she loves you very much."

I stood listening, and felt the warm wedge of tears building behind my eyeballs. How could I tell him Grandma was not there? Because I didn't see her was no irrefutable evidence he didn't see her. He was wearing a happy smile, and nodding his head as if he was listening to her speak. I just stood like a marble statue on display.

"Your Grandma is living in a heavenly place. She wants to know when I'm coming to join her," he said, and then quickly added, " I told her as soon as you get everything worked out at your school, I will come and join her."

The tears had reached my eyelids. I backed out the door. "Good night, Grandma," I said, and closed the door. He was hallucinating, I thought as I walked back to the living room. I tried vainly to dam the tears, but they overflowed. I could still hear him speaking to Grandma in his bedroom as I walked into my bedroom and closed the door. My denial was no longer credible. Reality had raised its afflicted head to remind me that life is fragile, and that I must learn to cope with the fact that Alzheimer's disease was slowly and methodically taking control of my grandfather's mind and body, and there was absolutely nothing I could do to reverse the process. The clock was ticking. I reached for the journal, and started to read.

* * *

We were herded onto a truck and driven a short distance. The barrage of racial slurs continued until the truck stopped. I wanted to tear away my ski mask and blindfold to view the faces behind the voices insulting me and the others. When the truck stopped, we were led off and our ski masks and blindfolds removed. I couldn't see. A hot, blinding, white light made everything blurry. Slowly, I could make out grotesque figures moving around me like the fast-forward movement of a movie reel. Hands were touching me softly, as if searching for something to hold on to. My eyes began focusing, and the grotesque figures became Black men crowding around me. We were huddled together. No one spoke. I looked around. We were in a compound completely enclosed with barbed wire fence. Then I saw the bodies behind the voices that were spouting racial slurs. Most were young men trying to be soldiers. I felt sorry for them. It was a sad affirmation of the finality of Hitler's youth group members.

We were taken into a dimly lit building with two levels. Each level had a row of rooms with sequential numbers printed on each door. Each individual was forced to stand facing a door until the guard came along to open it. I was on the second level, and when the door I was facing opened, I was pushed inside.

It was not a cell like the one in Hamburg. No cell bars, but four bare walls. The only window was a small stained-glass panel that permitted some light to filter in. A light bulb, fixed on the ceiling, could be turned on and off only by a switch outside the door. The door was thick, with traditional "L" shaped handles, and a lock was built solidly into the door that could be opened only with a large key from the outside.

There was no furniture. No bed. No chair. A small wooden pallet, about three inches off the floor, and large enough to accommodate a man's body, was the only moveable object in the room. Paint had been splashed haphazardly over the cement walls in a futile effort to cover hairline cracks. In one corner of the room was a cement mound about five inches high, built around a hole in the floor. The mound had the sensuous shape of a stretched vagina. I gathered it was my toilet. I could sit on it, stand over it, or lay on it with fantasies of having sexual intercourse. A small pipe protruded from the wall with a control valve clamped to the end. Underneath the pipe was a cement trough leading to the vagina, for flushing, I thought. But, when I turned the faucet on, it was dry.

Sounds coming from the next room caught my attention. A man's voice was murmuring as if uttering a prayer. His voice would rise and then mumble down until it was inaudible. I thought of praying because I knew we were all doomed. But I really didn't know how to pray. I hadn't been to church since I was a young boy going with my father. He always prayed and I would instinctively move my lips—mimicking him, but nothing came out. Or, at the table when my father blessed the food, his words came so fast that I couldn't understand their meaning, and I often wondered if God understood the sudden outburst of words ending with an abrupt reach for the nearest plate of food. But the sound of praying next door was soothing, and I lay down on the hard pallet and fell asleep.

I was awakened later by the hollow sound of the lock on my door. Someone was about to enter. I sat up and waited until the face of a Black Man appeared. His head was lowered and his eyes diverted mine as he sat an empty cup, some bread, and a piece of sausage on the floor. He disappeared and the key turned in the lock.

I picked up the cup first because I was thirsty, but thoughts of the dry faucet offered no consolation. But when I turned to look, crystal drops were bouncing off the cement. I turned the faucet fully on and a thin stream of water seeped out. I was convinced it was a biblical miracle, and not the result of someone turning on a master switch. It was a sign that everything would be okay. It was encouraging.

I ate what I assumed was my breakfast since the light filtering in through the stained-glass panel was from the sun, and not the yellow glare of powerful spotlights.

With my stomach full from the bread, sausage, and lots of water, I sat with my back against the bare wall and refused to think about death, torture, or anything I knew the Nazi regime was capable of. The question of why I was there was no longer relevant. Whatever was going to happen, would happen, I reasoned. Instead, I thought about Hilda—the wonderful warm nights, and happy days playing music—Wolfgang, and my apprenticeship as a farmer. Those days were, without a doubt, the happiest days of my life. I began recalling specific days, nights, events, and the remembering process kept my mind active and my heart beating normally.

Besides the constant praying of my next door neighbor, and the cadence footsteps of the guards as they patrolled each level, it was quiet. Several times I heard what sounded like a chilling scream, but it was not repeated and I placed no importance to it.

I wanted to wash myself. I had no soap or towel, but I had water. So, with the cup, I gave myself a brief shower using my shirt from the newly issued blue and white striped inmate's uniform, to dry my body. I felt clean and refreshed.

Hearing my door being unlocked, I waited for the face of a Black Man to appear with my lunch. Instead, a guard loomed in the light of the hallway motioning for me to come out. The guards rarely spoke. They were experts at giving explicit signals with their hands or the menacing barrel of their rifle.

When I passed the guard standing by the doorway, he kicked me in my buttock. My mind raced back to the guard in Berlin. But I knew if I attacked this guard, it was sudden death for me. He held his rifle at the ready. I sucked in my pride and kept walking in the direction he was pointing.

I was pushed into a small office and told to sit. A lone chair stood in the middle of the floor. I sat. Minutes later, I was joined by six men dressed in white coats, looking like a medical team from a hospital. Each carried a large writing pad and a chair. They gathered around me and began asking questions in turn, beginning with my birth and progressing through each phase of my life. Their focus was primarily on my music training and abilities, and my passion for track and field. The discussion lasted several hours. They were cordial and professional. Some of my answers provoked laughter that shattered the mounting tension.

When I returned to my room, lunch was waiting: cold stew, or soup, with bits of vegetables, meat, and a piece of black bread. I ate with my fingers, absorbing the liquid with thick pieces of bread and jamming it into my mouth, ignoring the foul taste.

I thought about the interview. They must have been doctors, maybe psychiatrists. They had been kind and seemed impressed by my background. I felt relaxed, but I didn't want to fall into a false sense of security. I had to keep focused on the raw reality. I was a prisoner. Why, I didn't know.

The next day, I was ordered out of my room again by a different guard.

When I passed him in the doorway, I braced myself for the kick. It didn't happen. I looked back to the young guard, and he must have understood the bewildered look clouding my face. He smiled briefly.

This time I was taken in a different direction. The buildings in the compound were separate, but joined by a closed-in walkway between each building. After a short walk we approached two guards standing rigid beside limp, red and white flags with the black Nazi emblem barely visible. Behind the guards was a sign *"Kommandant"* hanging over a doorway. My guard saluted his fellow comrades, turned and marched away. One of the two guards led me inside and saluted the frail-looking soldier seated behind a mammoth desk. The soldier behind the desk returned the salute. Making a precision turn, the guard walked out.

"Have a seat," the soldier behind the desk said in English.

I was shocked. He was a soldier of the Third Reich—maybe an officer—and Germans were overly proud of their language. "Be careful," I told myself. "Maybe it's a Gestapo trick."

"I'm Kommandant Fink," he said. "I've been reading your record, and find it very interesting." He stood up and walked around in front of his desk. He was a typical German soldier— tall, blond, blue eyes, but it stopped there. This soldier's left arm was missing. The left side of his face had been restructured, and he limped on his left leg. But the way he stared at me with a smile courting his lips, I knew he wasn't Gestapo, because *smile* was not a part of the Gestapo's demeanor.

"What is this place? And why am I here?" I asked, trying not to stare at his deficiencies.

He sat on the corner of his desk and his left leg didn't hang naturally, as if he had no muscle control. "Lets talk about you, first," his smile widened, "Your record says you play several instruments, including the piano. What type of music can you play?"

"Just about everything," I tried not to boast.

"Go over there and play something." He pointed to the upright piano in the corner. My eyes bulged and my heart raced. It looked like a Black Madonna waiting for me to give proper respect. I wanted to get down on my knees and kiss the pedals. As I sat on the stool, the black and white keys smiled warmly as we renewed our friendship. I played excerpts from classical composers, then drifted to Irving Berlin and show tunes. Then, I did something I knew was not acceptable in Naziland. I played jazz: Duke Ellington, Stan Kenton and ended with Fats Waller.

When I looked back he was smiling broadly and waving his hand in the air.

"You're good! Come!" He motioned with his hand.

From the crystal cannister on a table behind his desk, he poured two glasses of clear liquid. I knew instantly it was *Schnapps* (German whiskey). He passed a glass to me and raised the other glass upward in his hand, "*Prosit!*" he said with a smile, and downed the contents of the glass. I hesitated, because I'd never learned how to drink the white, burning liquid without choking. I tried to remember what Wolfgang once told me, "Don't taste it. Just open wide and pour it down."

I did, and it worked until the liquid reached the pit of my stomach. When I bent over coughing, he laughed, "You were born in Germany, and you can't drink *Schnapps*? Sit! sit." He sat in a chair opposite me. "I use to play the piano," he said, and the yearning in his eyes told me he was a lover of music. "From a very young boy, I played. Now, I can only play half the keyboard." He pointed to the stub of his left arm.

"That's okay." My voice sounded without my permission, but I was thinking how Hilda and I used to play when she was my teacher. She'd played the right side of the keyboard with one hand, and I played the left side with one hand. He was looking at me as if I'd just given him the surprise of his life. "Come over to the piano," I said. He was hesitant, but when he sat down on the right side of the piano and pressed his hand down over the keys, and I answered from the left side of the piano, he smiled and his lips trembled with excitement, like a kid acknowledging the discovery of a new toy.

The next day we repeated the routine. He was having fun and was extremely friendly, which made me relax, and for a brief period forgot I was a prisoner. Our conversations were always embellished with glasses of Schnapps.

"Where did you learn to speak English?" I asked during one of our conversations.

"It began in *Hauptschule* (high school), and continued when I went to the university. My mother and father attended medical schools in England and America. So, English was always spoken around our house. I also read a lot of English books. How did you learn English?" he asked.

"Same way. My father and I always spoke English at home, and I listened to lyrics from songs by American singers."

" When I saw on your record that you spoke English, I just had to talk to you." He reached for the cannister and refilled our glasses. I could sense he was a lonely man, and it was odd that he was finding a friend in one of his prisoners.

"What happened?" I pointed hesitantly to his missing left arm.

"Oh," he grimaced, "that was a horrible experience I want to forget." He stared at the shirt sleeve folded in half and clipped to his shoulder.

"But will you ever forget?"

He looked at me and his eyes were warm with a hint of sadness. He dropped his head. Immediately, I wanted to withdraw the question, but when he raised his head and looked directly into my eyes, I knew he was ready to release whatever it was that made him sad.

"I was taken out of the university, where I was studying to be an architect, and placed in the army with the engineers." He spoke with a quiet eagerness, as if he were talking to an old friend. "Months later, I was sent to Russia. One day, my unit was moving through the Russian countryside when we met a heavy snow storm. We camped for the night. The next morning we were completely covered with snow, and it was still falling. My commander ordered me and two other soldiers to go find a landmark so we would have some idea of where we were. For several hours we trudged through heavy snow until we spotted a small village. I made a map as we retraced our trail back to where we left our unit. When we got back they were gone. They had left us!" His voice rose as if he still couldn't believe it happened. He poured down another shot of *Schnapps*. "Can you believe it?" He looked at me. "They left us out in the damn snow with nothing but our clothing and rifle. We were going back toward the village for shelter, when one of the men fell. The snow was falling so fast and furious I lost direction. We tried carrying the fallen soldier, but soon we became exhausted. Then the second soldier fell. I kept walking until faintly I saw what appeared to be a village. The snow was blowing fiercely into my face, sticking to my forehead, and sliding down over my eyes. I saw the village again, then images and white blurs gathered around my body.

"Fortunately, someone from the village found me and took me inside to thaw out. I had fallen on my left side. My face, left arm, and left leg were frozen. I remember being tied to a table, and a piece of cloth soaked with some foul tasting liquid, stuffed into my mouth. I watched in terror as a man with an axe, or machete, slammed down on my leg like he was cutting a piece of firewood. Because I was tied so securely, the only movement was my eyeballs as the pain seared my brain. The same procedure was applied to my left arm until darkness descended and I could no longer see.

"The villagers were primitive people who lived off the land. Perhaps I was the first human being they'd ever seen from the outside world. But they took good care of me; nursed me, and treated my wounds. There was no communication, except a warm smile. It was refreshing to be among a culture that had no aspirations of being the best in the world, or controlling the world's resources. They just lived day to day and were happy." He stopped and held his breath deep inside for a few seconds, then exhaled with determination.

"One day, when I had almost recuperated, with the exception of my face, German soldiers came through the village. They took me, plundered the village, and destroyed it, killing everyone." He looked at me for an answer. I tried to show my sympathy.

"They were innocent people, with uninhibited caring and compassion for a human life. As we left, and I watched the buildings exploding and soldiers firing at civilians as they tried to flee for their lives, I wondered why in the hell was I wearing the uniform. We weren't soldiers—just butchers. Anyway, I was sent back to Germany; spent many months in a hospital."

"Why are you still in uniform?" I asked.

"Yes, that was the final nail in my coffin. I thought I was going to be released from the army, but my father, who was a chemist with the IG Farber company—they made poison gases for the military—thought I needed to keep my mind active, and the military was the proper place. So he convinced someone in the upper echelon of the military to keep me in the army, and find me a job close to our home in Stuttgart. I wound up here in Mannheim."

"We are in Mannheim? What is this place?" I tried once more, feeling he was ripe for exploitation.

"You'll find out soon enough. I can tell you this. Once you come to this place, you will never leave."

I tried reading into his statement and didn't like my conclusions. He wasn't as soft as I thought he was.

"I have a plan for you," he said.

"Escape?" I said hopefully.

"No. The guards here have nothing to do when they are not on duty. Some are too young; others are seasoned soldiers. It would be good for morale if you could entertain them each night in the Kantine after they finish dinner. The music would be good for them ... and for me. What do you think?"

"Do I have a choice?"

"No."

When I returned to my room, I tried to unravel the mystery of the place I was being held. The more I thought about the Kommandant's proposition, it clearly suggested that this could be my only chance to find out what was going on. I was so immersed in my thoughts that I hadn't noticed the quietness coming from my neighbor's room. It was the time of day he usually did his prayers. I placed my ear flat against the cold, cement wall to hopefully pick up some movement or sound. Nothing. Then I heard the scream again. This time, one long scream that died slowly.

116

Oh, God! I shuddered. Was it torture? I curled up on my pallet and slept.

The next morning, a different black face brought breakfast. He tried to force a smile, but the mask of sadness was unyielding. I bowed in a silent gesture of thanks as he backed out of the room.

Later, a guard came to take me to practice music with the Kommandant. But instead of going to his office, we traversed through a part of the complex I'd not seen before. Then I saw the sign: *KANTINE*. The guard led me inside and pointed to the piano that had been moved from the Kommandant's office.

"The *Kommandant* want's you to practice for tonight," he said, forcing a smile as he backed away.

It was a large room, with long tables and benches on either side. This was the soldiers' dining hall, I thought. The soldier stood guard at the door as I walked to the stage. The piano had been placed in the center of the stage so I would be facing the audience from my right side. The *Kommandant* had planned it well for my opening night, but I didn't feel any enthusiasm .

I sat down and stared out at the empty seats surrounding the medieval-looking tables, and thought about the faces of men who were going to kill me. Yet, I had to sit and entertain them. It would be like playing at one's own funeral, I thought.

"Are you having stage fright?" It was the voice of the Kommandant entering the room. "Don't worry; they will love you." He placed his hand over his heart and did a curtsy.

I felt reassured, but was still uncomfortable. I thought about what Hilda always said before we went on stage, "Let's go out there and have fun."

"What should I play?" I asked.

"Play the same way you played for me the first time. They will understand your range and capabilities, and will ask you to play what they like. You know that music is the soul of a German. Play what he likes and he will drink, sing, and dance all night."

I understood what he was saying. I knew that from November to February, Germans celebrated *Fasching* (a time for music, drinking, and fun).

"When is *Fasching*?" I asked because I had lost track of time.

"Today is 13 November 1944. We are at the beginning of *Fasching*. That's why it's so important that we have music for the soldiers."

"May I have some paper and pencils so I can set up my program?"

"Sure." He motioned for the guard. Minutes later, the guard returned with sheets of paper, pencils, and a small briefcase. I thanked him. He smiled.

"Well, good luck tonight. I'm looking forward to your concert," the *Kommandant* said and hobbled out.

Back in my room, lunch was waiting. As I ate, it seemed as if the food tasted increasingly better each day. Was it just my imagination, or was the food really laced with drugs or poison that made it savory? My thoughts were valid, but my stomach was in violent disagreement.

With paper and pencil in hand, I tried setting up my program for the evening. I knew, because it was *Fasching* season, the soldiers would want to hear lots of old German *Fasching* songs. I knew some songs from memory, but I also knew they would sing so loud that I wouldn't have to play the entire song—just a melody here, and a few chords there, to keep the rhythm going. I would have no problem, I thought. But something else whispered to me that compelled my attention. I had paper and pencil. Why not write about what was happening to me. If written in English, I'd have a better chance of getting it to someone who could pass it on, and let the world know what was happening to Black men in Germany. The thought stuck and materialized. I decided to start from the beginning of my whirlwind circle of misfortune. I wrote until it was time to go to the Kantine. I felt good about my idea of a journal. It would be my legacy to the world. My only fear was I might not be around to write the ending.

When I entered the Kantine, the pungent aroma of *real* food permeated the room. All benches were filled with uniformed bodies and tables decorated with food and drinks. A few heads perked up as I walked pass onto the stage.

When I sat down at the piano, I noticed the Kommandant and several men in white coats seated at a smaller table. The Kommandant raised his hand as a signal for me to begin. I played the same assortment of music I'd played for him in his office. When I had finished, everyone stood and applauded. It was overwhelming.

They continued applauding until I sat down and started playing again. I played soft, relaxing music that floated above the noisy chatter of men greedily filling their bellies. As I looked out over the soldiers devouring the aromatic food my stomach was craving for, I noticed something unusual in the back of the room. Each time the door opened and food was brought out, I glimpsed a tall man dressed in white, with a high billowing cap. The most bizarre part was, he had a black face. My first thought was he had to be the Chef, and immediately realized why the food smelled so good. At the same time I wondered what was his position at the camp. Was he a prisoner?

When they had finished eating, the beer drinking, singing, and dancing began. I played *Fasching* songs, and once they started singing, I could hear several different groups singing different songs as if in competition. I took a break when I saw two young men in white bringing me food. I sat in divine awe of a whole baked chicken, boiled potatoes, and red cabbage. I prayed.

The music, singing, and wild frolicking continued until the lights began blinking at intervals. The soldiers filed orderly out of the Kantine. Many came to shake my hand. The Kommandant and the men in white also came to shake my hand. Several of the men in white were among the group that interviewed me. I wanted to scream, "what's going on here?" But the Kommandant interrupted my delirious thoughts.

"Follow me," he said.

He led me to a room in the back. As I walked through the door I saw an array of pots and pans, gleaming with cleanliness, adorning the walls. The floor, oven, and everything in the kitchen had been scrubbed to a polished sheen.

"Jacques! Where are you?" The *Kommandant* yelled in German.

A tall, thin, Black Man emerged through a door that was too low for his head.

"Yes, Kommandant Fink." His German sounded more French than German.

"Jacques, I want you to meet Hermann. He will live with you and work in the kitchen until it's time for him to play music each night."

"Yes, Kommandant Fink." He looked at me, and I knew intuitively that I was an unwelcomed intruder.

"See you tomorrow, Hermann," the *Kommandant* said as he left the kitchen.

"Come!" The lanky man said, while mounting stairs to a room over the kitchen.

Glancing around the room, I had a comforting feeling I'd just been taken off death row. The room was triple the size of my room and had two cots, with blankets, along each wall. A toilet, with a *real* stool and shower, was concealed behind sheets hooked to rods suspended from the ceiling. He pointed to the cot at the far side of the room. I walked pass a window with clear glass and rushed to look out. It was the first time I'd seen the outside since the night they removed my blindfold. I had a view of most of the compound, but guards and powerful lights were the only objects identifiable. I saw two buildings at the far end of the compound, but there wasn't enough illumination for me to identify what they were.

"What are they doing out there?" I turned to Jacques.

"You don't want to know," he said in his best German.

"Why?"

"It's best you not know."

"Are they torturing Black Men? I've heard the screams."

He looked at me and I could feel his obvious aversion for me. "You know why that cot was empty? He pointed to where I'd just flopped down. "He was my assistant in the kitchen. He too was obsessed with what was going on in those buildings out back. So, one night he decided to sneak down there with the help of a guard who was his friend. He was shot to death. It turned out his friend had been unexpectedly replaced by a new guard, I stretched out on the cot wanting to scream with frustration. It was as if my entire body and soul were succumbing to a total lack of motivation for survival.

Then I heard music—jazz, and the unmistakable voice of Louis Armstrong. I looked up. Jacques was holding a small record player on his lap. He was winding the machine with a crank, while smiling and shaking his head wildly in the air. I rushed over, forgetting all my frustrations.

Later, we talked.

"Where you from, Jacques?"

"Zaire."

"How did you get here?" I asked.

"I was one of the African soldiers guarding the German and French border many years ago. I met a German girl, fell in love, and left the outfit. We went to Frankfurt to live. I found a job washing dishes in a large Jewish restaurant where she worked as a waitress. I learned the business of cooking, and the owner sent me to school to get my Master Chef papers." He smiled with the memory.

"You are a good chef, Jacques." It was a true compliment.

"Thanks. My Marie and I got married, bought a small house, had two children and then Hitler came to power. Everything began to change. People didn't like seeing us together; treated us like we had the plague of something. Then one day we came home and the children were missing, and no one would help us look for them. We never saw them again. My Marie lost her mind and was taken away. I continued working until *Kristallnacht*. The Nazis destroyed the Jewish restaurant and brought me here. They had just started renovating this place. I helped them set up the kitchen."

"You've been here since 1938?"

"Yes. Where can I go? Without my Marie, nothing matters. Once, I tried taking my life by drinking rat poison, but I didn't drink enough and the doctors saved me. You'd better go to sleep now. We start work in a few hours."

The cot felt like a full-sized bed with mattress. I snuggled up and fell asleep.

CHAPTER 13—THE EVACUATION

It was after the Christmas holidays that I noticed Grandpa was leaving more and more food on his plate. Secretly, I watched him while he ate, and to my horror, learned he couldn't feed himself. He could get the spoon or folk halfway to his mouth, then a shaky, uncontrolled twist would tumble the food back into his plate. And, at times, he struggled unsuccessfully to get food off the plate onto the fork or spoon. I also noticed a constant wet spot on his pants, as if he had spilled liquid in his lap or urinated on himself. The words *emaciated, incontinent,* and *immobile*, spoken by Dr. Simon, were suddenly important to me. I had no training as a nurse. The reminder of Dr. Simon's instructions—"If he shows any signs of being emaciated, incontinent, or immobility, you must commit him to a nursing home"—loomed over me like a tornado warning. I had no time to think; I had to act. I visited a friend who was a nurse at the local hospital. He promised to stop by and help me.

I watched with admiration as he tenderly coaxed Grandpa to eat. He was patient, caring, and professional. He also brought special disposable underwear for the incontinent condition. After watching several days, I was confident I could do it alone.

Grandpa didn't talk much about the journal anymore. He was more interested in telling me about his conversations with Grandma Lucy, and his most pressing concern was, "When will you be finished with your school program, son?"

Each morning before leaving for school, I'd wake him up, assist him in dressing, and help him with eating. I would return on my lunch break and change the disposable underwear, if needed, and give him some lunch. His previous resistance to help had disappeared, as if he had completely surrendered to the fact he was helpless.

The weight of Grandpa's illness and the music program were beginning to take their toll on me. To prevent my stress level from soaring over the abyss, I separated the two stress generating factors. When I was at school, I didn't dwell on Grandpa's illness, and when I was home, I didn't think about Mr. Saberstein and the music program.

The school's music program was making rapid and significant progress. After the ultimatum from Mr. Saberstein, I initiated an aggressive promotional campaign. I printed colorful flyers advertising a *new* music program, and used my students to help promote by word of mouth. I had given my students complete expression of their musical talents. We experimented with different types of music noting the fundamental difference in harmony, rhythm, and style. During lunch periods we had jam sessions, and kids crowded around our building to dance or just sit enjoying the music as if it were an outdoor concert..

In retrospect, I think the music, and the kids, kept me from being totally stressed out with Grandpa's condition. Each day, I told Grandpa of my progress with the music program. He'd smile and struggle courageously with his vocal chords to say, "I knew you could do it, son."

I don't think I could've done it without Grandpa's encouragement, support, and confidence. Even though it was weeks before spring break, the program was already a success. I had a long list of students waiting to take part in the school's new music program.

One day, I was notified to report to Mr. Saberstein's office. It was my first visit since he'd issued the explicit ultimatum. The door was open when I arrived. Filled with arrogance, I walked right in. The office was empty. "Mr. Saberstein!" I called to the closed door of his private restroom. "Just a minute." His voice resonated through the door. Then the growling sound of a toilet bowl flushing, the fizzling thrust of water running in a sink, and Mr. Saberstein emerged smiling and wringing his hands. He walked pass me and closed the door to his office.

"How is the most popular teacher in Central High?" His voice echoed with what I felt were impending accolades. My arrogance soared. It was my first time having a real-world success, and I thought my feelings were justified.

"Fine, sir," I said.

He sat behind his desk, his salesmanship smile etched on his face, as if he were preparing to sell me the moon at a reduced price.

"Just look at all these applications for your music program." He held up a stack of papers, "I knew the first time I looked at your resume I'd found the right man for the job, Herman." He leaned forward. "A principal is only as good as his teachers. If one hundred percent of my staff had your qualities, I'd be running for President of the United States." He let out a roaring laugh. "Now tell me, how soon can we go into band competition with other schools. I wanna kick some asses."

Leaving his office, my heightened state of arrogance had been replaced by anger. He had been so busy congratulating himself that he'd forgotten to thank me for a job well done.

When I told Grandpa about the meeting with Mr. Saberstein, his only comment was, "Wait until I tell Lucy tonight. She'll be so happy that you've completed your program."

As I sat listening to Grandpa talking to Grandma in his bedroom, I wondered if it was hallucination, or if her spirit was really there and only visible to him. I also wondered if it was possible for me to share the same spiritual encounter with my parents.

I drank a half bottle of champagne, congratulating myself on being what I knew I could be. I had made my first arbitrary step toward being an independent person, and I was satisfied with my progress. I had given up on Mr. Saberstein. He was an immutable fixture within the system, like plumbing to a new home. He would remain until the house was destroyed. Hearing Grandpa laughing in his bedroom, I knew he was happy.

So, in this harmonious setting, I picked up the journal, sipped from my glass, removed the bookmark, and began reading.

* * *

It seemed as if I had just fallen asleep when Jacques woke me up.

"Get up," he said, shaking me violently. "We have to make breakfast."

My job was to do whatever Jacques wanted me to do—which was almost everything—like breaking dozens of eggs in a large bowl, washing pots, pans, and scrubbing the floor each time a wet spot appeared. It was much harder than working on the farm, because I hated it. The only part I liked was when the time came for me to eat. I had my choice of food, and my appetite was insatiable. My once lean and muscular body was slowly developing a friendship with layers of fat around my midsection.

When the fun and frolicking of *Fasching* was over in February 1945, a wave of sadness came over the soldiers. I played lively music while they ate, but they were consumed with their own interest and fears.

The tides of the war was turning against Hitler, and warning sounds of air raids could be heard each night. Fear was clearly visible in the soldiers' faces as they hurriedly ate their food and rushed back to their respective guard posts.

One night, after I'd finished playing to an unenthusiastic crowd, the *Kommandant* approached me.

"Come with me," he said.

I followed him, but when he stepped out the door onto the compound, I hesitated. I knew that once outside that door I was fair game for a guard's bullet.

"Come, you don't have to be afraid. You're with me."

I rushed out and stood very close by the *Kommandant*. I knew the white stripes on my uniform would be illuminated under the powerful spotlights, and with each step, I felt a bullet tearing through my body.

"The end is near, Hermann," he said, looking in the distant where yellow streaks of light flashed across the night sky and exploded like fire balls.

"I received a letter from my father. He said all major cities in Germany have been devastated by air raids, and Allied troops are pushing into Germany. It will only be a matter of weeks before they take complete control of Germany."

He started to walk as he talked, and I followed closely, hoping the guards would recognize the dark uniform of the *Kommandant* before firing at the white stripes.

"Hitler, and many of his high-ranking officers are on the run, but they won't get far." He sounded very optimistic, and I thought it odd that he was about to be defeated, and possibly killed, yet he was in good spirits.

"What will happen to me and the others?" I asked, realizing I'd never had any serious thoughts about getting out of the compound alive. Now, my body was being rejuvenated and I could smell and taste freedom.

"I'm sure everyone will be released, along with all the other camps in Germany. That's why I wanted to bring you here, tonight."

I looked up and we were standing before the building that held all the secrets. After feeling secure in the new knowledge that I might soon be rescued, I suddenly had grave doubts about knowing what was inside that building.

As he unlocked the door, I could hear my heartbeat, echoing through my ears like the muted sound of jungle drums. I wanted to run, but knew it would trigger the already tense guards, and I would be shot. I followed him inside.

In trying to describe what it looked like inside, I could say it looked like an emergency room in a hospital, with rows of operating tables, glass shelves filled with surgical equipment, scalpels, scissors, and many strange instruments I'd never seen. Or, I could say it looked like a mortuary because of the quietness and uniformity. And, because there was the shape of a body lying on a stretcher wrapped in thick paper, and sealed with wide-band tape. The outline of the body was, without a doubt, that of a man.

"Sit down, Hermann. I need to tell you something before you start looking around," the *Kommandant* pointed to a desk.

My mind was still glued to the body on the stretcher as I pulled a chair from behind one of the steel desks and sat down. Then my gaze explored the framed tin structure, looking for any clue that would indicate what was going on. I looked for blood spots on the cement floor to support my theory they were torturing Black men. But the floor was immaculate. I looked for anything resembling equipment that might be used for torture; everything seemed normal.

"As you know, Hitler has his own ideas about race," the *Kommandant*'s voice grabbed my attention, "unfortunately, he has convinced most of my countrymen to share in his belief. The Nazis formulated most of their ideas from Nietzsche, a German philosopher, who advocated the existence of the *Ubermensch* (the man beyond, or superman). Nietzsche believed the *Ubermensch* to be perfect in mind and body: 'There would be no foe to match him in strength, agility, and intelligence. He would delight in battle, and the more he fought, the more insensitive he would become to pain. There would be no religious doctrines to disturb him—he would be happy in the consciousness of his own strength. Without mercy, strong, and contemptuous of others, he would learn to disdain manmade laws and manmade gods, just as man himself had learned to belittle the type of fear exhibited by lower animals for lions and tigers.' Are you following me, Hermann?" the *Kommandant* must have noticed how I kept glancing around at the least perception of a sound or movement.

"Yes sir." I answered with renewed interest. I didn't know where he was headed with Nietzsche, but I was thankful for the distraction.

"Hitler's hatred for Jews is based mostly on his jealousy of the powerful Jewish people. His dilemma is: how can an inferior race be so powerful? His only solution is to take away their power—destroy them. But he will never stop wondering what it was that made Jews so aggressive, so successful. Even his ill-fated experimentations will not give him the answer. Remember what I said earlier about Nietzsche and the superman theory?"

"Yes, sir." He was articulating something I'd never heard before, and it was slowly taking my mind away from my surroundings.

"The Nazis party took what Nietzsche said out of context. The superman theory wasn't meant specifically for Germany. Even though Nietzsche was born in Germany, he had no real love for Germans. In a letter he once wrote, he said: 'It seems to me that Germany has become a regular school of besotment. Water, rubbish, filth, far and wide. I beg a thousand pardons if I have hurt your nobler feelings by stating this, but for present-day Germany, however much it may bristle hedgehog like with arms, I have no longer any respect. It represents the stupidest, most depraved, and most mendacious form of the German spirit that has ever existed.'

"Well, to Hitler and his party, the ideas of Nietzsche was so close to their own warped conceptions that they appropriated them. Hitler envisioned an army—a race—made up of *Ubermensch*. He made that vision his ultimate goal. The 1936 Olympics was his opportunity to serve notice on the world that Germany had an army of Nordic German supermen for athletes. And, they were invincible. But a Black man from America came along and disputed his claim, creating another dilemma. Of course, he had no fear of the Black man, because the Black man had no economic power. But he couldn't ignore the fact that Jessie Owens ran all over his super athletes. He needed to know why.

"This camp was set up specifically to find the answer, and to find a safe way to extract and transfer any source of physical power to his soldiers without endangering the genetic make-up of his blue-eyed, blond, Nordic giants."

The *Kommandant* saw the way my mouth opened in total shock. I couldn't believe what he was saying. It sounded like the introduction to a horror movie, and I didn't like the feeling soaring up from my stomach.

"Guinea pigs? You mean... oh, God!" the words came out like bullets from an automatic rifle.

"Yes, the men in white are doctors who select the most probable specimen. But, in the beginning, it was merely a scientific study—a paper trail. Then Dr. Josef Mengele, was appointed head doctor for all concentrations camps by the chief of Gestapo, and the rules changed. Thus, the surgical experimentations began. Dr. Mengele orders were to breed the race of soldiers Hitler wanted. Here!" he tossed me a key, "open the door to that room directly behind me marked private."

Many images flashed through my mind as I tried to guess what was behind the door painted in dark red.

"Go ahead," he urged.

My feet were unsteady as I approached the door and inserted the key. My mind had stopped wondering and was now a total blank, but my instincts were telling me not to open the door. I felt numb, as if I were about to walk into a raging fire and my body was quickly insulating itself for the intense heat.

I pushed the door open and stood staring into darkness. A familiar odor—antiseptic greeted me. The onrushing scent filled my nostrils as I brushed the inside wall for the light switch. The overhead lights came on one at a time, as if they were all connected as a separate unit to the same switch. As the lights flickered on, my eyes widened at the astounding sight. It was like watching a horror film and the camera switches abruptly to a gruesome scene, and shock waves paralyze the viewer. I stood speechless, my hand covering my mouth to suppress the hysterical scream that was dying in my throat. The room was filled with glass tanks of various sizes containing parts of the human anatomy submerged in clear liquid. All around me were arms, hands, legs, feet, testicles, brains, hearts, lungs, knee caps, and some parts I couldn't recognize. The coloring on the arms and legs was changing, but it was clear to me those parts belonged to Black men. I backed away slowly, feeling the rebellious surge in the pit of my stomach. My only thought was to get away and suppress the queasy feeling inside.

I heard the *Kommandant* closing the door as I recovered from my hunched over position.

"I'm sorry, but I thought it was better than trying to explain it to you," he said. I stared at the man who was trying to be a friend, yet was butchering my brothers.

I was having mixed feelings. I hated him, yet I liked him. He'd been kind to me. But that expanse between friendship and hate was rapidly shrinking.

"Why couldn't you have stopped this? You are the *Kommandant*!" I lashed out at him.

"I have no real authority here," he said. "This camp and all concentration camps are controlled by the SS and Gestapo. They send us orders and we must obey them. Some of the older soldiers here work for the SS. They wouldn't hesitate to kill me if they suspected I was not carrying out my orders."

On the way back to our building, the *Kommandant* pointed to another building isolated in a far corner of the compound.

"That is where the remains are cremated. The ashes are scattered over the fields as fertilizer."

I was silent as we walked back. I kept thinking of the screams I'd heard and the apparent agony those men had gone through before dying. The image of that room—those tanks with body parts floating in white liquid—had been etched on my brain, and I knew it would never be erased. The constant rumbling noise in the distance, and the hopes of an impending rescue that would end the senseless butchery, made it easier to climb the stairs to my room.

A few days later, I was awakened in the early morning hours by rapid gunfire, explosions that shook the building, and voices yelling commands as footsteps thundered through the building. I peered through the small window in our room and saw the tin building exploding in flames. I thought immediately of the flammable liquid in those tanks and the body parts.

"Come on!" Jacques was pulling my shoulder. I turned, grabbed my clothes, and followed him downstairs into the basement, which was a stockroom for his kitchen supplies. We sat in silence, listening to what sounded like a full-scale battle going on over our heads. After several hours, the gunfire ceased and loud bellowing voices were heard. The voices were speaking English. Americans or British, I thought. But after hearing the voices more clearly, I knew they were Americans. I wanted to rush upstairs and greet them, but a sad realization stopped me—I was a German ... a Black German, nevertheless, a German. I was the enemy. Then I heard footsteps directly overhead. Someone was walking around in the kitchen. The banging sound of pot and pans falling to the floor caused Jacques to twitch, as if they were destroying his personal property.

"Hey man, look at all this Goddamn food," someone yelled. I knew it was time to act.

"Hello! Hello ... We're down here in the basement," I yelled. There was silence.

Then, "Hey, Sarge! Someone's down in the basement speaking English. Sounds like an American." Silence again.

"Yes, I'm a prisoner." The basement door opened slowly and light erased the darkness. Rifle barrels peeked into the basement and Jacques and I clutched each other waiting for a barrage of bullets.

"Are you American?" a voice asked.

"Yes," I replied, which came as a convincing response.

"Are you alone?"

"No. One other prisoner is with me."

"Okay, come on up with both hands on top of your head."

I told Jacques to follow me and we walked up the steps.

Several rugged white soldiers stood around the room with rifles pointed at us.

"What in hell is going on around here with all these Black folks?" One of the soldiers remarked.

"Come over here," the only soldier without a rifle pointing at us, beckoned with his finger. "Put your hands down. Are you a soldier?"

"No sir."

"Then what the hell you doing here?"

I didn't answer.

"What's you name, boy?"

"Hermann."

"Can you speak German?

"Yes sir."

"Good! Then come with me while I interrogate these Kraut bastards." They believed me, I thought. They think I'm an American. I looked to Jacques who was still trembling. I tried to convey to him that everything would be fine. Following the sergeant, I was all smiles. But my jubilation faded when I thought about the *Kommandant*. He was the only one who really knew the truth. I had to talk to him. I knew he wouldn't deliberately expose me.

"Sir!" I said to the hulking figure marching ahead of me. He stopped.

"I'm a sergeant. Don't call me sir!"

"Yes, sergeant."

"What do you want?"

"Sergeant, do you know where the *Kommandant* is?"

"Yes, that cowardly Kraut is in his office."

"May I see him?"

"Yes," he smiled, "but he won't be talking much. Come on outside when you're finished."

"Yes, sergeant." He seemed like a nice guy, in a rugged sort of way, I thought. When I arrived at the *Kommandant*'s office, the door was open and I walked in. Seeing the slumped figure behind his desk, I thought maybe he'd had one *Schnapps* too many. But as I moved closer, the sight stunned me. I stopped. Where the *Kommandant*'s head should have been was a mass of pulsating red flesh, with streams of blood oozing out and streaming across the desk. In his hand was a pistol clinging loosely to his fingers. I turned and walked away. He had found peace, I thought. He'd reached that point where he was forced to do what he had long wanted to do. I walked out onto the compound and saw Black prisoners huddled in one group and

German soldiers in another group. They were guarded by haggard looking American soldiers.

"Hey Herman," the sergeant called. "Come over here."

When I passed the group of Black men, their eyes searched mine for some evidence of assurance. I smiled, and a joyous roar of approval spread among them. I was going to be their liberator. But when I passed the group of German soldiers, they looked with eyes of betrayal. To them, I was an American spy. This feeling was later reinforced as I translated for the sergeant during his interrogation.

None of the Black men were interrogated after I repeated to the sergeant what the *Kommandant* had told me about Hitler's plans.

While we waited for evacuation, Jacques cooked his last meal at the camp. It was a wild celebration as we ate, drank, and I played American music for the soldiers.

When the trucks arrived for evacuation, I rode in the Jeep with the sergeant and his driver. As we drove away, I looked back at the demolished tin building, smoldering, and felt profound sadness at the lives lost for a senseless experimentation. I clutched my briefcase, my only possession, and tried to think ahead.

CHAPTER 14—LAST ENTRY

When I awoke the next morning, I felt as if I'd had a horrific nightmare about a gun battle and body parts floating around. After stretching my eyelids, I realized I had fallen asleep reading that part of the journal where Grandpa was rescued from the concentration camp. Now that the stress and anxiety I'd had about reaching that particular part was over, I was thankful he didn't suffer any physical damage.

In fact, I was so happy I wanted to let him know. So, before preparing breakfast I went directly to his room, knocked on the door and eased inside. He was lying on his back; his eyes wide open and staring at the foot of his bed.

"Good morning, Grandpa."

He didn't answer. I moved around his bed thinking perhaps he was looking at Grandma, and they were having a silent conversation. After circling the bed, I moved closer to him.

"How are you feeling this morning?" I placed my hand on his forehead and felt a paralyzing shock wave. My breath rose from my stomach and lodged in my chest. He was cold. I was afraid to take a closer look at his eyes. "He can't be_dead," I thought as my breathing returned. I searched frantically for a heartbeat, but when his head rolled limply to one side, I knew he was dead. I placed my hand over his eyes and brushed downward. Then I sat down and stared, with mounting compassion, at the last known relative in my family.

"I'm sorry you had to leave, Grandpa, but I know you're with Grandma Lucy, and you are happy," I said, feeling that through the mystery of death, he was listening to me. "I want you to know that I've finished the journal." Then it suddenly occurred to me that it wasn't quite finished. I rushed to my bedroom and came back with the journal. "Grandpa, I'm sorry. I didn't quite finish it, but we can finish it together. I pulled a chair alongside his bed and started reading aloud where I'd left off.

* * *

Riding in the sergeant's Jeep ahead of the column of trucks made me feel like a hero. I felt as if I had assisted in my own rescue and deserved to be riding up front. We drove some distance from the camp to another compound that was occupied by American soldiers. I was allowed to clean up and given a plain military uniform stripped of stripes, patches, or other military adornment. A new pair boots, socks, and cap fitted well. Then I was taken to a room where five men wearing military uniforms bedecked with colorful ribbons and shiny brass were waiting. At least one wore silver stars on his collar. They were seated around a long, brightly polished mahogany table. As I sat at the end of that table, they were speaking in whispers among themselves. At first I thought maybe they were going to give me a medal for assisting the sergeant. But when they stopped talking and cold eyes focused in my direction, I knew I was in trouble.

They took turns asking me questions, and their loud voices echoed in the room.

"What is you name?"

"Hermann Hoffmann."

"That's a German name, isn't it?"

"I don't know."

"Where were you born?"

I hesitated.

"Where were you born, Mr. Hoffmann?"

"New York."

"Where, in New York?"

"Harlem." My answers seemed to come from out of nowhere, as if I had been unconsciously programmed.

"What are you doing so far from home?"

"I was on a musical tour of Europe with my parents."

"What kind of music did you-all play?"

"Gospel." I could see the exchange of glances between them and it looked like they were believing me. But that didn't stop my knees from silently bumping each other.

"What happened to your parents?"

"They were killed a few years ago by the Nazis."

"Why didn't you leave and go back to America?"

"I tried, but couldn't get out of Germany. I lived on a farm with a German family until I was arrested." I was beginning to relax. So far my story was making sense, at least to me.

"Is that where you learned to speak German, with this family?"

"Yes sir."

"Tell us what you told the sergeant about what was going on at that camp."

I felt this was my chance to impress them. I told them everything the *Kommandant* had told me and added what I had seen in the tin building. The room was in silence as they debated in whispers. Then the man with the stars on his collar spoke.

"It's very strange that our men have interrogated all Black survivors of that camp, and not one of them knew anything about what you just told us."

I felt the tension building again. What were they trying to say—I made it all up?

"Can you explain that, Mr. Hoffmann?"

"No sir. Except maybe the *Kommandant* didn't tell anyone else but me."

"You expect us to believe that the *Kommandant*, a *Kraut* officer, who hated Jews and Niggers, would confide in your black ass? Give us a break." His remarks drew a scattering of chuckles, and I felt the hostility, like a steel band, tightening around me.

Studying their faces, I realized that if Hitler were seated at the same table, he would blend in with the five officers, and I would still be the odd ball in the room. I had to convince them I was telling the truth.

I quickly explained my relationship with the *Kommandant*, trying to point out that he probably trusted me because I overlooked his disabilities and helped him to enjoy playing music again. They listened intently as I tried to portray the *Kommandant* as a disillusioned human being trying desperately to find himself and his place in the world.

My little speech got their attention, and I think touched a few nerves.

They huddled together, smoking long brown cigars. I waited. Once again, I felt my life being threatened. This was the third time, and I wondered if it would be the last. I knew they could easily convict me as a German spy and shoot me. Nothing would be said. I would be just another casualty of war.

"Mr. Hoffmann," the man with the stars spoke again, "since we have no corroboration on your story about what was really going on at that camp, we've decided it never happened. Why you made up the story is immaterial. It never happened! That place never existed. You understand! Mr. Hoffmann?"

I thought about my journal before I answered.

"Yes sir. I understand."

"Now! As far as you are concerned, we're going to put you on a boat and send you back to New York and Harlem where you belong. And please, keep your black ass there along with the other coons, understand?"

"Yes sir."

He motioned for the white MP to take me back to my room.

As I lay on my bed clutching my briefcase, I thought it was just another humiliating defeat. They didn't want to believe me because secretly they agreed with what Hitler was doing. I tried to look on the bright side. I was alive. They'd spared my life. Maybe they felt guilty about the coverup and as a gratuitous gesture were letting me go free. For whatever reasons, they felt assured that no one would ever believe my story. I fought tears as I opened my briefcase and began writing.

The next day, I was driven by two military policemen to the town of Bremerhaven, where I was loaded on a ship with three different groups of passengers—refugees, white soldiers, and black soldiers. Each group occupied different sections on the ship.

I was given a Red Cross arm band, and was told I had to work my way to New York. My duties included assisting some of the Black soldiers who'd suffered severe wounds, moving those around in wheelchairs who couldn't walk, and keeping the recreation area clean.

I talked to soldiers from the South, North, East, and West. I wanted to learn all I could about life in the United States. America was going to be my new home, and I wanted to be prepared to answer questions if I had to appear before another group like those military officers.

I had no idea where in America I wanted to live. Most of the guys I had conversations with lived on farms. I knew I'd be happy working on a farm again, but a deep ache inside was a constant reminder that I deserved more. America was the land of abundant opportunities, and I was convinced there was a special place for me. For days I wrestled with my thoughts, and it was only after talking with a soldier named Jake, that I realized what I wanted most.

"New York City is the music capitol of the world, man," he'd said during one of our discussions about music. "East side, West side, uptown in Harlem, and downtown in Greenwich Village. You can find any kind of music that's ever been written or played."

Jake had convinced me; music was my salvation. I always had a yearning to spend the rest of my life in the blissful world of music. New York City would be my new home, I decided.

Jake was from Harlem, and for the rest of the trip across choppy waters, and rolling waves that made everything in your stomach rush up to your throat, he explained what the Eastside, Westside, Harlem, and Greenwich Village was all about.

"The Eastside uptown is where all them high-class rich folks live, in million dollar apartments—movies stars, queens, and kings. The only thing you and me can do there is empty garbage cans. Now, the Westside is a little different. Middle class working folks and lots of foreigners live there. It's an okay place to live.

"Greenwich Village is where writers, musicians, and the brainy crowd hang out. It's also the home of most of New York's queers and faggots. It's a swinging place where you can find anything you want.

"But the place to be, in New York City, is Harlem. The Mecca for all Black folks—the little Africa of North America. Everything you find separated on the Eastside, Westside, and downtown can be found all together in Harlem. It's all there, baby. I was born there, raised there, and will die there.

"They sent me half way 'round the world to fight somebody I don't even know. Shit. I didn't even shoot at nobody. From what I'm told and saw, there ain't no Black folks in Germany. So, what am I fighting for? To save some white bastard's ass so he can come to America, get rich, and hire me to clean his backyard. To hell with that shit, man."

When the ship reached New York, I was separated from the soldiers and placed with the refugees. We were taken to Ellis Island where, for three days I was interviewed, photographed, poked with immunization needles, and finally on the fourth day, was given a brown envelope with Immigration and Naturalization Service printed in bold black letters on the outside. Then I was told to take the ferry to Manhattan. Inside the envelope was a passport, social security card, information papers, and one hundred dollars in twenty dollar bills.

The address I'd given the immigration people as my new residence was 129th Street in Harlem—Jake's address. He'd told me to stop by when I got everything straighten out. But what I forgot to ask, and Jake never talked about, was how to get around in New York City.

While the ferry was docking, I thought about a song played by Duke Ellington's orchestra called "A-Train." The haunting lyrics said to 'Take the A-Train, 'cause it's the quickest way to get to Harlem.' Taxis were parked outside as I left the ferry.

"Excuse me sir," I said to one driver leaning against the hood of his gleaming yellow taxi. "Can you tell me where I can catch the A-Train?"

He looked at my new clothes and squeaky, uncomfortable high-top shoes.

"Going to Harlem, are you?"

"Yes sir."

"Hop in."

We rode for about ten minutes through streets flooded with people and traffic jams, then he stopped.

"Ten dollars," he turned to face me.

It was my first time in a taxi other than with my father in Germany. I couldn't remember ever seeing my father pay for the taxi ride.

"Ten dollars?" I repeated.

"Yeah, ten dollars, please." He extended his thick hand over the back of his seat.

"But where is the A-Train?" I asked.

He pointed to a green-and-white sign across the street from where we were parked. "Go down those steps," he said, "and wait until the train comes. Where you going in Harlem?"

"129th Street."

"Get on the first car of the train and get off at 125th Street," he said, his outstretched hand still waiting.

I paid him, thanked him, and scrambled out of his car. "I will never ride another taxi in New York City," I thought, as I rushed down the steps to the train station.

The woman in the booth stared at me in disbelief as I tried to figure out what to do with the special coin she'd given me. Only when I saw another passenger walk in front of me, did I realize the coin fitted into the machine that permitted me to enter the platform where the trains stopped. Filled with embarrassment, I refused to look back.

When I walked up the steps into bright sunlight at 125th Street, directional signs indicated I was only a short distance from where Jake lived. Looking around, I noticed a marked difference between what I saw during my brief taxi ride and what I was seeing in Harlem.

Everything I'd read about Harlem, and from listening to Jake, gave me the impression Harlem was the Mecca for Black people in New York. But from my view—the buildings, streets, and people—had the squalid appearance of a South African ghetto. People stared at me as if I were certainly out of place with my ill-fitting clothes and tattered briefcase.

Standing in front of the apartment number Jake had given me, I hesitated to knock. Loud music blared through the door, muffling the sound of voices. I knocked, feeling I owed Jake for sharing with me the knowledge about New York City that I'd used successfully to fool the immigration people.

"Yeah!" A voice sounded from inside.

"I'd like to speak with Jake," I said, feeling someone was observing me through the small round hole in the door.

"Jake!" the voice yelled, "someone's here to see ya."

Minutes passed and I felt the urge to take off running. Then the door opened slightly.

"Herman! My man," Jake's voice resonated through the small opening in the door, "Come on in, man." He struggled to disengage the door from the chains and bars connected to it. "Everything okay?"

"Yes, I got cleared by immigration."

"Good. I have a few friends here. We're celebrating my return from the war." He began beating on his chest as if he were the hero and had won the war single-handed.

He led me into a smoke-filled room where several people sat in groups, passing around what seemed to be a hypodermic needle, while others heated something over an open flame.

"What can I get you to make you feel good, man? I got some of everything."

I thought for a second, but when I saw the needle penetrating the swollen vein on a woman's arm, I knew instinctively I was in the wrong place.

"Coke ... how about a coke?" I said.

"Coke? I got plenty coke. How you wanna use it?"

"I'll drink it," I said. My eyes were glued to the strange behavior of the groups who seemed totally unaware of my presence.

"Drink it? Man, that's bizarre. You cats in Europe is cool," Jake said as he flounced through the bodies slumped around the room, "I'll be back in a few, man."

I turned and walked briskly to the door. The chain and bars clanked as I moved them aside to squeezed through the opening. I closed the door tight behind me and walked swiftly back in the direction I had come. "My first day in New York City was having a quaint beginning," I thought, as I approached 125th Street.

On 125th Street, I stopped in a restaurant, chose a table in a corner, and scanned the menu. I thought about Jake and wanted to kick myself for not seeing that something was wrong with him on the ship.

He wore no stripes or other military insignia on his uniform. He had no apparent injuries, and he didn't associate with the rest of the soldiers. Jake was a drug addict, I thought, and was probably booted out of the army.

"May I take your order, sir?"

I looked up into the gentle face of a waitress. She was smiling. I was immediately warmed and felt relaxed.

She helped me select an enjoyable meal at the lowest cost, then made a humorous remark that I had the appearance of someone who'd just 'gotten off a bus or boat.' She suggested changes and additions to what I was wearing to blend in with the rest of the inhabitants. And, she recommended a place where I might find a room. She also gave me the address of her church and invited me to attend.

The place the woman recommended was the Harlem YMCA on 135th street. I was given a room, and I settled in with my briefcase and two colorful shirts I'd bought on 125th street to embellish my appearance. I checked my funds and realized I needed to find a job.

In the YMCA cafeteria, I met many people—mostly black—from different parts of the world: West Indies, Africa, England, France, and they were astonished that I came from Germany. I felt odd because of the sudden astonishment. What I didn't know was Germany, to the rest of the world, was an all-white society. Subsequently, some avoided me, but others continued to talk and through them I found out where to find a job.

After my introduction to New York City's subway system, with my precarious ride on the A-Train, I felt like a regular New Yorker when I boarded the crammed morning train to 35th street downtown and the Garment District. I was told that people were hired off the street with no questions asked.

I had the appearance of, and felt like, a freshly packed sardine as I emerged from the subway car that reeked of after-shave lotion, perfume, and a variety of other disorganized odors.

It seemed like a million people were rushing from underground and spilling out onto the streets of Manhattan. I didn't know precisely where to look for a job, so I began following people who looked as desperate as I did. I walked up one street and down another for hours until I spotted a cardboard sign swinging in the breeze, "Help Wanted," it said in hastily printed letters. I ran across the street and stood reading it to decide what to do next. Suddenly, I was bumped from behind and when I turned, the sign was going through the door and into an elevator, clutched possessively by a burly man.

The next day, I returned to the Garment District more street-wise. When I found a help-wanted sign, I seized it and held it firmly under my arm as I walked up the stairs to the floor and the firm indicated on the sign.

The firm manufactured women's outer garments: dresses, skirts, and coats. The room full of women were animated as they sat in front of sewing machines that hummed with precision. A smaller group of men, with measuring tapes and small hand-held electric saws, were hunched around long tables piled high with fabrics. They looked like wood cutters with gleaming saws, trimming limbs from fallen trees.

I was hired to keep the floor clear of excess trimmings and to make deliveries in a three-wheeled boxed cart with a tall "L" shaped rod that, when garments were hung, looked like a clothes closet on wheels. It was new for me and lots of fun. I delivered gowns to fashion shows, elaborate showrooms, and sometimes got a sneak-peek at the models. But the job was hectic. Everything had to be delivered within minutes. It didn't pay much, but I was able to save a few dollars a week, after my rent, food, and transportation.

Then one night, when I came from work, I heard music emanating from the basement of the YMCA. I discovered they had a "Little Theater," and some group was rehearsing for a musical show. I hadn't played music since the concentration camp, and my body vibrated with joy when the sound of music instruments blending together in a song resounded in my ears.

I joined the group as assistant music director. I felt my life in New York was taking off. We produced several musical productions at the YMCA to benefit charities, and I got my name in the newspaper. It was a wonderful feeling. A job in the Garment District and the YMCA being so impressed with my music abilities that they made me music director, were positive signs that I was indeed moving up.

I should have been happy, but that ache deep inside kept telling me I wanted more. It was an insatiable longing that worried me. In the meantime, I became infatuated with the sound of music that could be heard on weekends, emanating from a nightclub across the avenue from the YMCA.

From Friday nights through Sundays, Small's Paradise reverberated with the sounds of jazz and blues. A parade of limousines and well-dressed people were constantly arriving. I would stand outside listening to the sounds and could imagine myself playing to the crowd of rich and famous people.

I was so obsessed that one weekday night I conjured the nerve to walk in and pick a seat at the bar. In the middle of my beer, which was all I could afford, I saw the piano standing on a small stage, smiling at me. I immediately asked the bartender if I

145

could play it. He became frighten by my furious outburst when he said no and quickly summoned a burly man who took me firmly by the arm over to the piano.

"Just what is your problem, sir?"

"I just wanna play this piano, mister," I said meekly.

"Are you a musician?"

"Yes sir."

"Let me see your card."

Card! This was new to me.

"You cannot play music in a commercial establishment in New York City, unless you're a member of the musician's union," he said.

"I'm sorry, sir, I didn't know. I just came from Europe and I—"

"You just came from Europe?"

"Yes sir."

"Sit down and show me what you got." He gave me a firm pat on the back and disappeared.

I looked out at the scattering of people and began to play. As I became more and more immersed in my music, I noticed the club was filling up with people. I received a thunderous applause each time I finished a song, and that motivated me to keep playing until the club closed at 3 a.m.

As the club was closing and I was getting ready to leave, a man came over and introduced himself as the manager. He said it was his night off, but he had been called in to hear me play. He offered me a job three nights a week and agreed to help me get my union card.

I overslept the next day and was late for work in the Garment District. I was fired, but it really didn't matter. I was making more money working three nights a week at Small's and part-time at the YMCA than I'd made working one month in the Garment District.

My whole world was changing. Each night that I played, a lovely lady would sit alone at a small table watching me. After several nights, I found myself playing just for her. A strange, angelic glare surrounded her. I wanted to talk to her, but she was out of my class. I could hardly afford to buy one of those exotic-looking drinks she always ordered. She would send me requests—all different types of music—and I would do my best to honor her requests.

Then, one night during my break, the manager hurriedly escorted me to her table and introduced us. Her name was Lucy. And that was the real beginning of my life in America with my soul mate.

LAST ENTRY ON THIS DAY 16 JULY 1948

I closed the journal. "Well, Grandpa, we finished it."

I got up, covered him with a sheet and left the room. It was the final closure on the traumatic life of one remarkable Black man, I thought. But I had a deep feeling that something else was needed to make an absolute and final closure.

CHAPTER 15—THE JOURNEY

I had Grandpa's body cremated. Being the only family member left, I didn't see the need for an elaborate funeral. We didn't really have any friends in Hempstead. After Grandma Lucy's death, Grandpa became withdrawn, refusing to allow anyone else to come into his life. He even severed his relationship with his friends and colleagues at Juilliard. When I sent the notification of his death to the school, only a few responded with condolence.

The cremation was part of my plan to put an appropriate closure to my grandfather's life. My plan included scattering half of his ashes on Grandma Lucy's grave—I felt they were already together—and personally scattering the remaining ashes somewhere in Germany. I could not overlook the fact that he had been *born* in Germany.

In order to make my plan work, I needed the help of my old friend Sigrid. I wrote her a detailed letter explaining what I wanted to do and asked if she could help me. The details included:

a. Going to Germany at the end of the school year.

b. Visiting a concentration camp in Germany (Buchenwald).

I wanted to get a general understanding of what it was like to be a prisoner in a concentration camp. Since Grandpa indicated in his journal that the camp he was in had been categorically denied by American officers as having never existed and was possibly destroyed, I was skeptical of ever finding it near Mannheim.

c. Visiting Hamburg and the town of Wilhelmsburg, where Grandpa had been born. I would probably scatter the remainder of his ashes in Wilhelmsburg.

d. Visiting Berlin to locate the site of the 1936 Olympic Games where Grandpa was first introduced to hate by Hitler.

e. And finally, making a concentrated effort to locate any residual evidence of the existence of the special camp near Mannheim.

Seven days after I'd mailed the letter, I received a telephone call from Sigrid. She was delighted that I was coming to Germany and promised everything I'd listed in the letter would be accomplished. She requested I send her my flight itinerary. My plan was set in motion, and I waited impatiently for the end of the school year.

The school year ended on a positive note. The kids in my music program were happy. Mr. Saberstein was happy because he had won his first band competition. I tried to be happy, but losing Grandpa and being all alone made it very difficult. I was hoping that seeing Sigrid again and putting a final closure to Grandpa's memory would free my mind and heart of the awesome responsibility as the last living relative of Hermann Hoffmann.

Three days after school had ended, I was sitting at Kennedy Airport waiting to board my flight to Germany. I'd watched the sleek Lufthansa jet being positioned at the loading gate. I felt a rush of excitement at the thought of visiting the place that I'd read so much about in the journal and of course seeing Sigrid again. Secretly, I was hoping she had reversed her lifestyle, and we could renew our relationship.

It was my first time in an airplane and I'd made it a practice, when I was in unfamiliar surroundings, to watch and do what people around me were doing. So, when I boarded the plane and a lovely flight attendant checked my ticket and pointed, I thought she wanted me to follow the passengers walking down the aisle matching their ticket numbers with seat numbers. Oddly, my ticket numbers seemed out of sequence with numbers on the seats. It was only after I'd reached what I believed to be the tail end of the aircraft, that I dared ask the person preparing food in a small alcove about my seat. She smiled and told me I was in first class, up near the entrance. With pangs of embarrassment slapping me, I struggled back to the front, found my seat, sat down and closed my eyes.

As the plane took off and I felt the smooth ascension, I realized I was leaving the United States of America. A sudden wave of apprehension gripped me, causing some ambivalence in my planned journey. It was a feeling that a child probably gets when leaving the safety and security of his home on the first day of school.

When the plane landed in Frankfurt, and I emerged into the arrival area, I heard a shrill voice, "Duke!" I turned and saw Sigrid running toward me; her arms outstretched, her mouth wide with a smile. She slammed into me; her arms coiled around my neck. "Oh, Duke, I'm so glad to see you," she cried.

Her body was slim, curled like a bent wire. I felt I could encircle her waist with one hand. My body was suddenly ebullient, as if it had just been plugged into a 500-watt power source. I savored the moment until I noticed the petite girl standing a few feet away. She was smiling up at me with my arms wrapped protectively around Sigrid. Then I remembered Sigrid's chosen lifestyle, and tried to return her smile.

Her skin, the color of smooth cinnamon framed her oval face surrounded by neck-length silky black hair—carefully groomed. Her eyes, like black almonds, were fixed on us as I reluctantly released Sigrid, and she slid down my body. I felt deflated, as if someone had just pulled the plug, and my life was slowly hissing away.

"This is Maria, my friend," Sigrid said. I noticed the word *friend* had a special sound. "She's from Paraguay."

Maria extended her hand. After our brief handshake, she stepped swiftly back and reached for Sigrid. They embraced, and at that moment I knew it was a sincere commitment. They were inseparable, and I would have to love them as one.

When we reached her car, I stopped in awe of the sleek, silver Mercedes. It reminded me of the red Mercedes sports car Sigrid's father drove in New York. Sigrid saw the awestruck look on my face.

"Oh, it's not mine," she laughed, "It belongs to my mother. She thought we'd be more comfortable in this since we have so far to travel."

"And what kind of car do *you* have?" I said in jest.

"Maria and I have a convertible BMW just for two." And with their hands joined, raised them in a salute to the two of them. I regarded this gesture as an unequivocal declaration to their commitment.

"How wonderful it must feel to be so euphorically in love," I thought, as I eased into the immaculate back seat. As we drove away from the airport, I struggled with my pride and decided I had lost Sigrid and must accept it like a man.

Sigrid pulled into the entrance of the Marriott Hotel in Frankfurt and stopped. "I've reserved a room for you for tonight," she said. She gave me a sheet of paper. "This is your itinerary for the next few days. Get a good night's sleep and we'll pick you up early tomorrow morning."

"Okay." I uttered as I crawled out of the car. "What time tomorrow morning?"

"I'll call you. You meet us right here."

"Okay."

We waved as the car sped off. I stood staring after my two jean-clad chauffeurs with raised halters and I thought, "They must be angels of happiness."

I glanced at my itinerary:
Day one... . Buchenwald
Day two... . Hamburg
Day three... Berlin
Day four... . Frankfurt

My first night in a foreign city was one of sleeplessness. I didn't know whether it was the room service's lasagna, which definitely didn't taste like the lasagna my grandfather made, or just feeling homesick. I sat by the large window in my room on the 65th floor and surveyed the Frankfurt skyline. It was beautiful, but it only brought back memories of the infamous New York City skyline that took one's breath away.

My colleagues at school talked about Frankfurt being the New York City of Europe. My only thought was that Frankfurt's underdeveloped skyline had a long way to go to even come close to Manhattan. Somewhere in the unsettling debate, I fell asleep.

Sigrid and Maria were prompt the next morning, and as we left Frankfurt and entered the Autobahn (Germany's super expressway), I felt Sigrid was trying to qualify for the Indianapolis 500. She darted dangerously in and out of traffic, and hurled insults at those drivers who tried to impede her dominance of the left lane. I tried, with little success, to view the beautiful German countryside with its colorful patches of cultivated farmland, villages, and towns looming in clusters across the landscape—showcasing their salmon-colored rooftops—but everything became a blur and I felt it safer to tighten my seat belt, close my eyes, and pray.

I was awakened by the soft sound of Sigrid's voice. Somewhere in my sleep path I'd had a passionate dream about Sigrid. Seeing her beautiful face in my dream haze, I thought it was just an extension of my dream.

"Duke! wake up." It was Sigrid's voice again.

I opened my eyes, and the red and white letters *ESSO* in the background brought me painfully back to reality. We were at a gasoline station.

"You've been sleeping for hours," Sigrid said. Two beautiful faces were smiling at me from the front seat.

"Want something to drink?" Maria asked.

"Yes, a Pepsi. Do you have Pepsi in Germany?"

"Come on," Maria laughed. "We have everything in Germany." She dashed from the car.

"Where are we?" I asked Sigrid.

"Weimar," she said, and opened the door to step out. The guy filling the tank quickly diverted his gaze from Maria struggling at the soda machine to Sigrid. I immediately felt the role of protector and jumped out the opposite side. I leaned over the top of the car and flashed a warning signal to the guy. My lips didn't move, but my burning gaze and the distortion of my facial features must have been persuasive. He immediately dropped his gaze to the gasoline hose.

"Weimar? Are we still in Germany?" I asked. Maria had bounced back with the cool, refreshing Pepsi.

"Yes," Sigrid answered, "This place, to Germany, is like Philadelphia is to America."

"How so?"

"The Constitution you live by was started and completed in Philadelphia. Our constitution was started here in 1918. The only difference is yours is still in effect, but ours died when Hitler came to power."

As the car sped away from the ESSO station, I looked back and several other men had joined the guy at the pump, and they were staring in our direction. I had to fight a smile as I thought about the movie "Driving Miss Daisy." I could be "Mr. Daisy."

Sigrid, our expert and knowledgeable tour guide, pointed out historical sites in the town of Weimar,.

"Goethe lived there," she pointed to a modest house that had been recently repainted.

"You mean Goethe as in *Faust*?" I said.

"Yes," Sigrid replied with a loud giggle. I knew she was remembering the times we spent in Central Park reading *Faust* as if we were rehearsing for a Broadway production. Our favorite scenes were *Faust* and *Marguerite*. Sometimes our readings were so loud that we drew a crowd.

"Goethe was born in Frankfurt, but came to Weimar to live. He wrote *Faust* while living here."

Maria seemed as excited as I was to be driving through pages of history. The town of Weimar still carried some residuals of war—bomb-scarred buildings—but the narrow, cobblestone streets and ancient structures gave me the feeling I'd been caught in a time lapse somewhere in medieval Europe. I was mesmerized by a town with so much ancient history.

However, my serene feeling disappeared as we drove up a steep hill and stopped in front of the entrance to Buchenwald Concentration Camp.

A tall, bronze monument introduced visitors to what awaited them up the winding road that snaked through dense vegetation and forest. The car moved slowly. The scene of quiet and reverence in the car made it appear as if we were part of a funeral procession. I was experiencing the same feeling I'd always felt when I visited the cemetery of my parents and grandparents— I was on hallowed ground.

For Maria and me, it was our first time visiting a place where so many people had perished, and the impact was clearly visible on our faces.

Sigrid had visited the camp several times as a student.

"This road was called the *Road of Blood*," Sigrid said, indicating the winding road we were traveling. "Over there," she pointed to a railhead, "is where the trains brought prisoners to their final destination."

I sat up abruptly, feeling maybe it was a mistake to come. I didn't like the emotional tugging inside.

Sigrid pulled into a large parking area jammed with tour buses and private cars. It was comforting to note that a lot of people were curious about the legacy of Buckenwald.

"This area was the SS parade ground. And these buildings," Sigrid pointed to the parking lot and a group of three-story barrack-type buildings, "were the barracks for the SS troops." The yellow buildings, with salmon-colored roof tops, had been well maintained, and a few had fresh coats of paint. "Several of these barracks are for students on field trips who wish to spend the night. I stayed two nights in the first building," she said proudly.

I couldn't help but notice the abrupt change in Maria's demeanor; I suddenly missed her bright smile and vivid animation. She moved as if she were hypnotize, and reacted only when Sigrid guided her. I hadn't known her long enough to interfere, so I kept my mouth shut.

Our first stop was the entrance to the actual campsite. A tower stood over an iron gate and connected with ground-level buildings on either side. A high barbed wire fence extended from the end of each building to encircle the camp. I kept staring at the clock built into the tower with it hands set at three o'clock. The time was incorrect.

"That's the time this camp was liberated back in 1945," Sigrid said.

Walking underneath the sign that read, *To Each its Own*, through the iron gate, and onto the actual compound, I tried to feel what Grandpa must have felt when he was taken into that compound and the blindfold removed, or the millions of others who passed where I was standing and were pushed into an ocean of helplessness. But I realized it was not a spontaneous feeling one could just conjure up at will. It was a feeling only those people, at that time, could understand.

I stared at the vast area that had been cleared of barracks which were once squalor homes of the inmates. It was now acres of flat land covered by dark gravel and tar. Subdued memorial stones for victims of "special camps" were placed in several locations. I moved to each stone hoping to find the word *African* or *Black*—anything that would tell the world "we suffered too." There was nothing. It supported the theme of all the movies I'd seen, and all the literature I'd read—there were no Africans involved in the Holocaust.

The emotional part of our tour began when we approached the crematorium. Signs outside in German and English requested everyone to observe silence in honor of the dead. I heard Maria sobbing. Sigrid was holding her and whispering. I was the first to enter—through the pathological department where experimentations were performed, through the commemoration room, and a room filled with hundreds of urns containing ashes from some of the more prominent victims. Maria could no longer contain her sobs and completely broke down. Sigrid motioned for me to continue and escorted Maria out of the building.

I walked down the steps into the cellar, which had been used for executing and storing bodies. The only thing missing between the place I was in and the one Grandpa described in his journal, was the glass containers with body parts. Otherwise, the awesome feeling I had was what I assumed he had. I felt overwhelmed with emotion and wanted to leave. But I had to see the ovens. Grandpa never described the ovens—only the building housing the ovens.

I moved upstairs to a dimly lit room. Fresh flowers were scattered on the floor in front of the ovens. I stood staring at a row of black steel plates encircling large round holes bored into a thick, brick wall. The holes were charred inside and had no floor. Whatever was thrown inside was burned as it descended to the bottom of the wall. In front of each oven was an iron cart mounted on rails. I envisioned a body being thrown into the cart, the steel door of the oven yanked open, and the cart rammed against the open door, dumping the body into the hot, engulfing flames. I closed my eyes and walked away. Outside, the warm sun and fresh air couldn't halt the suppressed emotions. I wept openly as I walked back up the hill toward the entrance. I had seen enough.

Maria had recovered. She apologized to me.

"I'm sorry," she said.

"It's okay, Maria." Looking into her serious dark eyes, I knew she was deeply troubled.

"Tell him, Maria," Sigrid urged.

Maria looked deep into me, and her eyes were mesmerizing.

"When I was a little girl, rebels invaded my father's farm in Paraguay," she said, "They sexually molested me, and with my mouth taped so I couldn't scream, murdered my entire family. Then they piled the bodies up like stacks of timber and burned them. They left me sitting, bruised and hurting, to watch my family being reduced to ashes."

"What happen to you? How did you get away?" I asked.

"I managed to free myself and wandered deliriously around in the jungle until someone found me. I was placed in an orphanage and later adopted by a German missionary couple."

I reached for her and held her close. I could feel her body vibrating as she tried to suppress her sobbing.

Leaving the camp, Sigrid pulled into a parking lot.

"We need to have a good closure to this visit, and I think this is just the spot," Sigrid said.

The spot was a huge tower built on a hillside overlooking miles and miles of open German countryside, towns, and villages.

"This is a national monument built in 1958 to honor all who died at Buckenwald," Sigrid said.

The monument was surrounded by hundreds of stone steps that led downward toward the German countryside. Halfway down those immaculate stone steps was a large statue depicting the figures of men, a woman, and a child, in various poses of protest. At least one of the men had a black face, but I couldn't tell whether or not it was because of its prolonged exposure to the weather. At the end of the steps was a circular stone stadium that was a miniature of the coliseums of Rome during Caesar's reign. Carved into the circular wall were engraved commemorative plaques of the different nationalities that perished at Buchenwald.

My heart fluttered as I moved from plaque to plaque searching frantically for some identifying acknowledgment of Blacks who had suffered. After reading the last plaque, I walked back up the mountainous steps feeling angry and disappointed.

We drove in silence until we reached the Autobahn. Sigrid turned on the music and looked back to me, "Hamburg, next stop," she yelled. I could feel the Mercedes accelerating, and I knew Sigrid was ready to take off. I checked my seat belt, crossed my fingers, and closed my eyes.

It was early evening when we arrived in Hamburg. A light rain was falling giving the city a pellucid sheen. There was something excitingly notable about this city, and I immediately thought of Central Park in New York City, but this city was a composite of steel, stone, water, and vegetation—a virtual tropical island.

Maria had made hotel reservations from the car while I slept. So Sigrid drove directly to the Inter-Continental Hotel. We check in, had a late snack, and said good night.

Since I had slept on the trip, I sat by my hotel room window and stared down at the wonderful city of Hamburg. The fact sheet from the tourist bureau said it was the second largest city in Germany. In my own thoughts I added, "and probably the most beautiful." It was a wonderful concept, "A city in the park;" an architectural masterpiece. I tried to think of other cities I'd visited in America that had a similar concept; I couldn't think of any. However, I knew that some volunteer groups were planting trees in Manhattan but "it would take a much larger effort to bring it up to the standards of Hamburg," I thought.

The next morning we ate breakfast. Then off to Wilhelmsburg—my grandfather's birthplace. I carried the pouch containing Grandpa's ashes tucked protectively inside my jacket.

We took the *S-Bahn_*(inter-city train) to Wilhelmsburg, because Sigrid thought we'd be able to get a better view of the city from the train. And it was a magnificent view. I bounced around with excitement like a kid on his first trip to the zoo. When the train stopped at the Wilhelmsburg station, a somber feeling hovered over me. And when we stepped from the train, that feeling expanded. Deep inside I believed I was having an ancestral connection to the town of Wilhelmsburg, which made it very personal to me. We started walking through the city. I had no address. Grandpa never spoke of the specific street he lived on. As we walked, I felt a creeping sensation that I had more with me than just Grandpa's ashes. I felt Grandpa, himself, was with me.

The city was actually an island. You could walk only so far in any direction and you'd invariably end up by the water. It was a quiet town, with large industrial and residential areas. Modest homes and high-rise apartment buildings gave the appearance of a thriving community. Children, enjoying the summer sun, romped in the streets. These were the same streets where my grandfather felt as if he was "the only child left in the world." There was something I noticed that brought an immediate smile to my face. The children resembled the student body at Central High School—a small representation of the United Nation.

After hours of walking and trying to determine where to scatter Grandpa's ashes, Sigrid suggested we scatter them in the waters surrounding the town.

We were walking through a park on our way to the river, chattering and laughing like a group of happy teenagers, when we heard a voice calling, "Hello! hello."

We turned to look back and an elderly man in a motorized wheelchair was waving to us. He was traveling on a parallel path a few yards behind us. Evidently he'd been following us. He beckoned to us. When we approached him he was wearing a wide smile. He was a frail little man and seemed to be strapped securely to the wheelchair. He gave us a visual inspection; his gaze traveling from head to toe.

"Are you British or American?" he asked.

We looked at each other and shared a brief laugh.

"I'm German, he's American, and she is Paraguayan," Sigrid introduced us. "And you?"

"I'm Norwegian. I thought you were tourists. We don't get many tourists anymore."

"How long have you been here?" I asked. He was speaking good English, and I felt that I could participate in the conversation.

"About ... fifty ... or so years." He spoke slowly, as if he were having trouble remembering the years.

"Maybe you know my grandfather, Hermann Hoffmann. He was born here in 1925."

"Hoffmann ... I knew some Hoffmanns," he looked hard at me, "but I don't think I knew your grandfather. I worked on the docks, so I don't think we would have had the chance to meet socially."

I felt deflated.

"Why did you come to Germany to live?" Sigrid got back into the conversation.

"I was a Merchant Marine. We came into Hamburg port often. I met a German girl and got married.

"And the war, did you have any problems during the war?" Sigrid asked.

"Oh, I had no problems. I continued working on the docks until the bombing and the fire storm."

"Fire storm?" I cut in. I didn't remember reading anything about fire storms in Grandpa's journal.

"Yes." He looked at me and for a brief second he was Grandpa, leaning back in his wheelchair happily telling his story. "When the British bombed Hamburg, some of the bombs were incendiary. They ignited fuel depots and coal storage facilities that quickly developed into a fire storm which burned out of control for days. Most of the deaths occurred from the fire."

"My grandfather had a bad time during the war," I said, feeling it wasn't necessary to go into details. "He died a few months ago, and I came here to scatter some of his ashes, but I don't know exactly where he lived."

He reached for my hand and held it tightly. I could feel the hardness of his bone structure. "That's wonderful. I know your grandfather is happy knowing you care this much." His body trembled. "I just wish my children and grandchildren cared as much. Since my wife, Anna, died, all they care about is trying to put me in a nursing home. Since I refuse to go, they buckle me in this chair each day and put me out on the street. I think they're hoping that one day this wheelchair will get out of control and run into the river, and I don't mind telling you that sometimes I wish it would, too."

I looked at Sigrid and Maria. They were passing tissues between themselves. I kneeled beside the wheelchair and pressed his brittle hand between mine. I felt painful memories of the many times I'd held my grandfather's hand or helped to guide food into his mouth.

"Don't you worry. Someone cares," I said. He looked at me. His glazed eyes searching my face. "You have lived a long time, and obviously God cares and knows the reason why you are still with us. He has a plan for you. Did you ever think of that?" He shook his head and tears bounced off his furrowed cheeks. "Don't you let anyone make you feel you're not wanted— because you are. And always remember, God loves you."

With his free hand, he touched my face tenderly as if to make sure I was real. "Thank you," he said, and his wrinkled face allowed a smile. "You know, the best place to scatter your grandfather's ashes is at St. Michael's church in Hamburg." His eyes lit up as he spoke. "Go up into the tower and let your grandfather glide down to Wilhelmsburg." I looked at Sigrid. She nodded.

Sigrid and Maria hugged and kissed the little old man who's spirit seemed to have been rejuvenated by our visit. As I walked away, I looked back and knew I'd never forget his face.

While waiting for the train back to Hamburg, Sigrid translated information about Wilhelmsburg from a pamphlet: "The large island of Wilhelmsburg, between the North and South Elbe, was the property from 1673-1927 of the Dukes of Luneburg-Celle. Because of its low-lying situation, this area suffered particularly severe damage as well as the greatest number of casualties in the catastrophic floods of 1962."

I was listening to Sigrid, but everything after the word *Dukes*, just flew pass me. Grandpa had talked about his father having been bought off a slave ship in the late 1800and raised by a Duke. The Dukes owned the island until 1927—two years after my grandfather's birth. I smiled. Pieces of the complicated puzzle were slowly coming together.

St. Michael's church is a landmark of the city of Hamburg. Ships entering or leaving the port of Hamburg are greeted by the green patina-covered tower of the church situated on a ridge above the harbor in the southern part of the city. The church has been destroyed, or severely damaged on several occasions, but each time it was fully restored.

Riding the elevator to the tower some 500 feet above the city, I had a feeling of reverence and peace. The moment I stepped out on the viewing platform, I knew it was the right place. The magnificent panoramic view embraced the whole of Hamburg.

"Wilhelmsburg is over there, Duke," Sigrid pointed, and she and Maria walked hurriedly away.

I stood facing the island. The wind was calm. I reached for the leather pouch containing the ashes, and as I eased it from my pocket I felt a lingering warmth where the pouch had rested against my body. I had a sudden impulse to keep them.

"Grandpa, I hope you're satisfied with what I'm doing." My voice was slightly above a whisper, but I felt as if I were speaking over a public loudspeaker, "You said that working on the farm with Wolfgang and Hilda was a happy time in your life ... since I have no idea where the farm was located, or even the street where you were born, I'm releasing a part of you from this platform. I hope it will complete the cycle of your existence. It's the closing chapter of a proud and resilient Black man— Hermann Hoffmann—my grandfather."

I unzipped the pouch and slowly turned it upside down. The ashes drifted downward, but a sudden gust of wind came up and held them aloft, and they wafted away. I smiled and felt an esoteric sensation of lightness, as if I was standing on the moon.

Sigrid suggested we celebrate by shopping, and she promised me a surprise that evening.

I learned that Sigrid and Maria were frequent visitors to Hamburg. Several times each year they played music with a symphony orchestra or small group ensemble. They traveled all over the world and refused to work unless they were playing in the same orchestra.

That evening, wearing my newly purchased, overly expensive trousers, shirt, and sandals, we strode through the streets of St. Pauli's Reeperbahn, Hamburg's Red Light district, looking like happy inhabitants of the local culture. I thought of New Orleans, Los Angeles, San Francisco, and New York City all thrown together into one pot. It was all there—everything to satisfy one's wanton desires.

Walking up and down the narrow, crowded streets with Sigrid glued to one side of me and Maria the other side, I felt like a king with two of his most beautiful maidens.

My surprise for the evening was a visit to the, Cotton Club. It was an image of the Cotton Club in Harlem during the 1920s that I'd read so much about. The name was also synonymous with Duke Ellington and other big bands during that era.

Sigrid continued to work her magic and persuaded the manager to let us play while the regular band was on break. I was delighted. We played as a trio: me on piano, Sigrid on violin, and Maria on bass. It was wonderful to play jazz with Sigrid again as we continually challenged each other. I thought of Grandpa playing in the same city with Hilda and Gesla and it made the evening more enjoyable.

We slept late the next day, but were on our way to Berlin by midday.

We arrived in Berlin just in time for the mass exodus of workers scrambling to get home.

Traffic clogged the streets; belligerent horns blasted while drivers fumed in despair. It was truly reminiscent of New York City at the end of a workday.

Among the first things I learned about Berlin were: It was the largest city in Germany, was officially named the New York City of Europe, no longer a divided city, and had the dubious distinction of being one of the most dynamic and exciting cities in the world.

In trying to compare Berlin with Hamburg, I had to admit Berlin was more of a metropolitan city, with healthy green trees up and down the boulevards, and main streets. Almost everywhere I looked a tree stood waving in the breeze. What was apparently missing were the crystal cool lakes that snaked through the city of Hamburg. Berlin had all the characteristics of New York City—people, litter, and a general unkempt appearance.

We didn't have much time to spend in Berlin because we were weary from the previous night in Hamburg. I was on a mission and that was utmost in our minds. I had to visit the site of the 1936 Olympics to see what vibrations I could feel from the infamous shunning scene between Hitler and Jessie Owens. But, Berlin was certainly not the type of city where one said hello and goodbye in the same breath. It was provoking and made one want to linger.

Although Berlin was her home, Sigrid made no mention of stopping by her house. My thoughts were that Maria was creating a wedge between Sigrid and her mother. It was none of my business, so I dismissed the thoughts.

Sigrid insisted I see parts of the old East Berlin and remnants of the Berlin Wall before going to the Olympic Stadium. I immediately noticed the difference between east and west Berlin. East had an immaculate appearance, but fewer people on the streets. The answer was: they'd all thronged to the west when the wall fell.

About one city block of the wall was left standing as a memorial to the few hundred people who were shot trying to scale it to escape to the west. It was not the formidable structure pictured in newspapers and movies. It looked weak and defeated, with holes punched through the hard stone and steel, and now covered with graffiti.

Leaving east Berlin, we passed the infamous "Check Point Charlie" hut, where American soldiers faced down Russian soldiers daily until the wall fell. Although the original hut had been dismantled, a museum had risen with a motley collection of wall paraphernalia including sentry boxes, chevron posts, booby traps, rolls of barbed wire, and pieces of the wall.

We traveled through the towering Brandenburg Gate, which my grandfather described in his journal during his visit to the Olympic Games. Once the structure stood as the Arch of Peace. In 1933, Hitler used it when the Nazis' torch-light procession through the arch was intended to mark the beginning of the 1000 year Reich. Later, it was used as a humble tollgate, marking the city's western boundary. Today, it symbolizes the reconciliation of east and west Berlin.

Finally, we drove down tree-lined boulevards with overflowing sidewalk cafes and expensive shops. Then we entered Olympia Boulevard, the street that lead to the Olympic Stadium. My heart fluttered, my eyes stretched to see the stadium. It was like waiting excitedly to see an eclipse.

And suddenly it loomed before us. The brief description Grandpa gave in his journal was quickly magnified. Tall, white poles, some visibly in need of repair, stood stolidly on each side of the huge concrete square—the size of two football fields. Obviously, they were meant to hold the flags of competing nations during the 1936 Olympic Games. The area must have also served as a parking lot, although I wondered how many people had automobiles in 1936.

Sigrid parked the car and reached for my hand.

"Take your time, Duke. Maria and I will wait here for you." She squeezed my hand.

I walked up to the gate that marked the boundary line, and stood staring up at the two mammoth pillars stretching the Olympic Rings flag—hanging limply between the pillars—like a clothesline weighted down with damp wash.

The man at the gate asked for money. I extended my hand full of German coins. He took what he needed and smiled.

I was still about 200 yards from the entrance and it suddenly occurred to me that *everything* about the stadium was oversized. Even the statues, on both sides of the stadium of two athletes greeting each other, were enormous, and projected an immediate feeling of power and greatness.

My first thought was that perhaps it was part of Hitler's message to the world: "Germany is bigger and better."

I glanced around and discovered I was the only visitor. I proceeded to the entrance and walked inside. The air was cool and damp. It was a quiet and ghostly scene. It looked and felt like the relics of a medieval dungeon. Heavy stone beams supporting the upper seating decks were cracked, exposing rusty steel rods. It was frightening to walk under the massive slabs thinking they might collapse at any time. Some efforts had been made to repair the cracks, breaks, and huge gaps in the structure but it seemed futile.

I walked up to the railings and stared down at the center of the stadium. I thought about Grandpa's description: "It was a massive stone structure that resembled a gigantic spaceship hovering for takeoff. Red cinder bricks glistened in the sunlight. A plush carpet of green grass bordered each side of the structure, and inside, gray stones rose tier upon tier to encompass seats for over 100, 000 people."

The red cinder bricks were no more. Weather had changed their color, but the green grass and gray stones that rose up to the height of a two-story building remained.

I was alone in the stadium, but when I closed my eyes I could see all seats packed. I could feel the furor and anticipation of the crowd waiting for Jessie Owens. But the sudden sound of footsteps brought me back to reality. I was no longer the sole visitor.

I walked through scarred corridors, leaving only to see the Olympic swimming pool, still in use, and acres of well kept land used for other Olympic events. People were leaping off the high diving towers into the gigantic pool, and soccer and polo games were heating up in other areas.

At one end of the stadium was a commemorative area dedicated to the architects of the stadium, and a list, in bold print, of the winners, by events, in the 1936 Olympic Games. Jessie Owens' name was first and second on the list. I felt a sense of profound pride and gratitude. At last I had found some *acknowledgment* on my trip to Germany.

After walking three-fourths of the way around the circular stadium, I reached what I believed to have been the dais where Hitler and Jessie Owens had the brief confrontation. The entrance was locked, but I didn't let that deter me. I climbed over the railings and entered the area. Standing, facing out over the massive crowd, I tried to imagine Jessie Owens coming to face

Hitler as the winner of four gold medals—the champion of the games—and Hitler retreating doggedly back inside the press room. I tried to imagine the intense feeling Grandpa must have had at that moment, even though he was only a small boy. But, strangely, I didn't feel any hate or scorn. I felt what I thought was a normal reaction of being in a place rich in a historical context, and a memorial to the Black athletes who competed in the 1936 Olympic Games. Then I realized that many years had passed, and it was time to put a closure to the unfortunate incident. But I persisted because I had a desperate desire to feel something—to reunite with the past—to be a part of my heritage. But I was happy, because I felt nothing. I took one last look out at the empty seats and decided it was time to go.

I walked outside the stadium and immediately saw the bell. Grandpa had described the huge bell tolling just before the game and thousands of pigeons simultaneously released carrying flags of competing nations. Now, the bell sat alone, propped up on a wooden deck, unable to ring ... silent ... as it should be.

When I slid into the car, there was silence. Then Sigrid spoke.

"You okay, Duke?" I nodded.

"Good. Let's go home."

I sat back in my seat and felt a genuine sense of peace and happiness. I was so elated that I didn't bother to fasten my seat belt. I felt invincible.

* * *

Sigrid called the day following our Berlin trip to tell me she had information about a military prison near Mannheim that could possibly be the site of the old concentration camp. She said that she and Maria would pick me up for dinner, and she would explain.

If Frankfurt had more rivers and lakes flowing through it, I would compare it favorably to Hamburg. Throughout the city of Frankfurt, trees and beautiful gardens were aplenty.

We ate dinner at an outdoor cafe. Balmy trees with wide green leaves fanned us, and hedges trimmed with an assortment of colorful flowers bordered the garden, emitting a spicy aromatic odor. Tropical and rare flowers were protected behind thin glass shields, and a small band played soft music from behind an illuminated background of flowers. It was a heavenly setting.

Sigrid and Maria were beautiful. Dressed in identical black gowns that slimmed down to their ankles with side slits giving a flashing glimpse of tanned thighs, they looked like the angels they were.

"Someone told me yesterday that there is a military prison near Mannheim," Sigrid said. "It belongs to the US Army and is the only military prison in Europe."

"Oh, God! What do you think?" I tried to shield my excitement.

"I don't know, Duke. You don't have much information to go on, other than the prison your grandfather was in was located near Mannheim. This may be a coincident. Maybe the army is using the site of the old prison. What have we got to lose? Lets go have a look."

"Okay!" She had convinced me. We slapped a high-five and enjoyed the rest of the evening.

The next day, Sigrid and Maria were waiting when I came out of my hotel. Excitement was racing through my body with thoughts of visiting the area where my grandfather may have been held as a prisoner. I wondered what kind of experiences I would feel. The Olympic Stadium experience was telling me to let it go, that my persistent desire to relive my grandfather's feelings and experiences was impossible. But I knew that the prison site would be the final chapter. It would bring closure to a very painful time in my life. It would permit me to move forward and build a life for Loukmann Hoff that would make my parents and grandparents proud. Most of all, it would leave an indelible legacy for the Hoff/Hoffmann family.

When we arrived in the vicinity of Mannheim, Sigrid followed the US Facilities signs until we drove up to a huge brown and white sign that told us we were on military soil.

"I don't see any sign about a prison being here," I said.

"Neither do I," Sigrid said, "but I know it's here somewhere."

Sigrid drove past the empty guard hut and it was just like seeing a movie about the military. Rows of uniform buildings—evenly spaced and identical in structure—greeted us. Most of the buildings were old and apparently had been inherited from the Nazis. We drove throughout the spacious installation looking for anything that would identify where the prison was located.

Finally, we decided to ask someone. We were told to follow the sign "Correction Facility." We did, and it took us away from the military population to an isolated area. At the bottom of a hill the huge, faded sign gave a warning: "Please turn back now, unless you are on official business."

Sigrid stopped the car. She looked back to me. I could see the fear in her eyes. Ahead, I could see only the top of a guard tower. I couldn't see any guards walking around the deck. My mind told me that since there were no guards in the tower, it wasn't a maximum security prison.

"Drive on," I said. I had come too close to be turned back by a sign.

"You sure?" Maria asked.

"Yes. It's okay. I'm on official business." I didn't have the slightest idea what I would do if we were stopped for trespassing.

"Okay!" Sigrid drove slowly up the hill, and suddenly the prison loomed before us—rows of gleaming white two-story buildings constructed in the form of a T. The bottom of the T being the entrance. The boundary wall was a high barbed-wire fence. Inside the boundary wall were several layers of thick barbed-wire surrounding the buildings. The sharp metal prongs on the wire gleamed in the sunlight like finely honed silver.

Sigrid drove slowly past the tower and parked in front of the entrance. I checked my passport, and got out like a diplomat. It was very strange and eerie. Nothing moved. No signs of life in the immaculate looking buildings. I glanced around, hoping to see someone I could talk to. I walked toward the bottom of the T.

Standing before the entrance, I tried to convince myself that this was the same place Grandpa had been taken—that inside this gate the prisoners had been unloaded from trucks and the blindfolds removed. Suddenly, the metal gate began to slide open. I was stunned for a second until I realized it was being operated from inside. I walked inside the narrow, fenced-in passageway and a very large military policeman was waiting for me. I am six feet, and he had to be a good two feet taller.

"May I help you, sir?"

"I ..." I stammered and reached for my passport. "... was wondering whether you could tell me when this facility was constructed?"

He eyed me suspiciously, and his gaze shifted to the silver Mercedes and Sigrid and Maria standing out in the sun.

"If I knew, I couldn't tell you, sir. Sorry." He gave me back my passport and walked back into his small office.

"Is there someone else who can tell me?" My voice was strong and I believe caught him off guard. He turned, and I thought I saw a smile breaking up his sourpuss expression.

"Drive back on main post and find the Installation Coordinator's office. They may be able to help you." The smile came through.

"Thank you." I returned the smile.

The sergeant at the Installation Coordinator's office was very cooperative.

"The Correction facility was built in 1963," he said.

"What about the rest of the buildings, they seem very old?"

"Most are World War II vintage," he said.

The sergeant was a Black soldier, and I felt safe asking the next question.

"What percentage of the inmates at the Correction Facility are Black."

He hesitated, then turned away.

"I'm ashamed to say, but I would guess between seventy to eighty percent." He dropped his head.

"Thank you, sergeant," I grabbed his hand, "you've been very helpful." I wanted to hug him, but my intuition told me soldiers don't hug one another.

On the trip back to Frankfurt, I debated with myself. The Correction Facility could very well have been the same place my grandfather had been held. I had no idea what was behind the rows of immaculate buildings and barbed-wire fence. Perhaps the old buildings were torn down and new buildings constructed in front of the old. Or, the military officers who interrogated my grandfather made sure the site was totally demolished. Whatever the case, it was sufficient to put a closure on it. However, if it was, in fact, the same place, and the percentage figures the sergeant gave me were correct, it would certainly be a very bizarre coincidence.

****

I stood at the entrance to the departure gate in Frankfurt's International Airport and received a separate goodbye from Sigrid and Maria. Each one ended with, "Goodbye, my brother."

I took one last look when I walked through customs and saw them waving. I realized I was no longer alone in the world. I had two new sisters who were Angels of Happiness. And I knew I would see them again.

End

About the Author

S. L. Williams was born in Georgia, and grew up in New York City. After receiving a BA and MBA from The University of Maryland, he worked for the Federal Government until retirement. Currently residing in Germany, he writes full time and his short stories have appeared in numerous national magazines.